HORATIO CLARE

Icebreaker

A Voyage Far North

VINTAGE

1 3 5 7 9 10 8 6 4 2

Vintage
20 Vauxhall Bridge Road,
London SW1V 2SA

Vintage is part of the Penguin Random House group of companies
whose addresses can be found at global.penguinrandomhouse.com

Penguin
Random House
UK

Copyright © Horatio Clare 2017

Horatio Clare has asserted his right to be identified as the author of this
Work in accordance with the Copyright, Designs and Patents Act 1988

First published in Vintage in 2019
First published in hardback by Chatto & Windus in 2017

penguin.co.uk/vintage

A CIP catalogue record for this book is available from the British Library

ISBN 9781784706791

Printed and bound in Great Britain by Clays Ltd, Elcograf S.p.A.

Penguin Random House is committed to a sustainable future
for our business, our readers and our planet. This book is made
from Forest Stewardship Council® certified paper.

MIX
Paper from
responsible sources
FSC
www.fsc.org   FSC® C018179

To my shipmates,
at home and afloat,
with love and thanks.

And through the drifts the snowy clifts
Did send a dismal sheen:
Nor shapes of men nor beasts we ken—
The ice was all between.

S.T. Coleridge,
The Rime of the Ancient Mariner

Contents

CHAPTER 1

Ghosts

LIKE A small luminous yeti in search of food I tramp
towards the centre of Oulu. Snow floods out of the
darkness, shoaling around the lights, settling deep on
the town. Nothing else moves. It is half past eleven on
a Sunday night and I am quietly, dizzily happy. Tomorrow
morning my ship comes in. In my violently orange coat,
warm as a bear's belly, I am ready for the ice. The ice is
close by. You can smell it, a hard purity in the cold.

The north seems a vast imagined surround, pine-dark,
duned with snow and specked with Arctic towns as
deserted as Oulu, their garrisons all stood down. They
are in bed all over Ostrobothnia now. They are in bed
across the water in Sweden and over the border in Russia.
Seven hundred miles south-west, beyond the Skagerrak,

the Danes must have finished their Sunday *hygge* ('to stay in with loved ones and enjoy an absence of stress'); around here, perhaps, the odd Finn is still practising *kalsarikännit* ('to get drunk at home alone in your underwear with no intention of doing anything else'). In the peace I experience one of those leaps of the heart, of love and thrill for the world, a euphoric gratitude for life and travel for which there can be no one word in any tongue.

Oulu is at the northern end of Finland's west coast on the shore of the Bay of Bothnia. The Bay is the northern armpit of the Gulf of Bothnia, which is the northern arm of the Baltic sea between Finland and Sweden. We are a hundred frozen miles short of the Arctic Circle. I am here to join Icebreaker *Otso*, the bear. *Otso* is coming in to change her crew and take on food and fuel. Tomorrow we go to sea. For ten days I am going to break ice with a crew of Finnish seafarers, mostly in darkness, certainly in snow.

For months I have been waiting for tomorrow, since the message came from Pekka, whom I knew a little at school. He was an angular, amused boy then, with that staccato way of speaking English the Finns have which lends itself to wryness. Last year he wrote to me, 'I just got an idea which might interest you, given your fascination with ships. Would you like to hear more?'

Pekka is press counsellor at the Embassy of Finland in London. He is charged with raising his country's profile in 2017, the centenary of the nation's birth.

'Would you like to travel on a government icebreaker? I think if you do the journey, something will come of it.'

A Finnish proverb says, 'The brave eat the soup, the timid die of hunger.' I have no great appetite for public relations trips but I did not hesitate: darkness, ice, Finland and a ship! Three days ago I turned up in London lugging a bag stuffed with thermals and layers and merino and a hat and an under-hat, mittens and under-gloves, these thumping army surplus boots and this ridiculous coat, to find I was thirty-six hours early for the flight.

Another Finnish proverb says, 'Don't jump before you reach the ditch.' 'A man comes back from beyond the sea, but not from under the sod,' says yet another. The first part of this last one is reassuring but the second is nonsense. I am also here because of a man under the sod who keeps coming back.

Pekka and I had someone in common: Thomas, an arresting boy who became a beloved man. Thomas was extremely tall; his thoughts and comments were terribly quick and his face was a satyr's, wickedly clever, the nose slightly lopsided, the impression a beautiful hotchpotch of narrowing eyes, high bones and round rumbustious jaw. Thomas could be an explosion of noise, ludic dash and charisma, or Thomas could be utterly attentive, searching your face as he listened to you, devoted to understanding what you were really trying to say. Thomas loved to solve problems. In his thirties he seemed to have cracked the problem of life. He lived in Switzerland with his family. He was engaged on a project which involved putting capital to work for charity: he was one of those people who habitually improve strangers' lives simply because they can. And then, one foggy day, Thomas fell on ice while skiing. He was in a coma for weeks.

Here is the strange thing. While Thomas lay between life and death my partner gave birth to our son, and as the baby began to be able to focus on the world, as its lines and depths began to cohere, and as Thomas slipped further away, I began to see in the baby's eyes, beyond all sense but there, and growing and focusing there, some blaze-bright light of will and life which I knew, which I had seen before in Thomas.

The turbulence of grief for my friend and my adoration of the child surely conjured this vision, a projection, but that is not how I experienced it. It was as though they were passing each other, brushing by each other, making some exchange in that region before and after understanding which is neither quite life nor death.

As Pekka and I planned this adventure, we spoke of Thomas, who connected us.

'It is amazing, the effect he has,' Pekka said. 'That he keeps having. It is wonderful.'

In my heart I feel that this is why I am making this journey and this obscure voyage. 'Something will come of it,' as Pekka said.

I will not know what that something is until this book is finished. But perhaps this is not a story about seafarers and ships, and Finland, and ice, and the dreams of worlds that are gone and others still forming, and nightmares of worlds melting, and the wilderness of an obscure and frozen sea, though it will surely be about these too. Perhaps it is really a story about gulfs inside, about inner uproar contained in silence, about the breakable and about that which cannot be broken. Perhaps this is why I am nervous. You meet yourself at sea in ships, and your ghosts too.

CHAPTER 2

Helsinki

YESTERDAY THE plane descended over a striated scape of snow and forest, frozen lakes and outcrops of rock. A century ago Finland was sundered in civil war, Reds against Whites, a vicious overspill of the Russian Revolution. The Second World War came in three parts here. First was the Winter War, in which the Finns halted a huge Soviet attack. In the Continuation War the Finns attempted to regain lost territory by joining the German attack on Russia, and in the Lapland War they turned on their former allies, driving German forces out of northern Finland. During the Cold War Finland opted for 'active neutrality', staying out of Nato for fear of offending Russia, a policy which continues to this day.

Since the last shots of the Lapland War a population of five million has produced a nation where the education system is among the best in the world, where women occupy 40 per cent of positions in a government ranked among the world's least corrupt, and where social mobility is strong, thanks to education. Until the 1990s the gap between rich and poor in Finland was narrowing; a banking crisis early in that decade reversed that, and the divides between the most affluent, the middle class and the poor have since grown. However, the Finns believe that decent lives should not be reserved for the privileged. Taxes are high, and Finland has recently become the first European nation to offer a sample of unemployed citizens a basic income which is not withdrawn if they find a job. A universal basic income may not be the answer to unemployment, but it is typical that Finland should be the first country to experiment with it.

If the measure of a place is its treatment of the most vulnerable, Finland is a world leader. This is the only nation in Europe which does not have a crisis of homelessness, the only one in which homelessness has declined – achieved by providing permanent housing for the homeless, rather than temporary accommodation.

Seen from Britain, Finland might as well be floating somewhere above the crisis-ridden muddle we currently call reality.

Forehead pressed to the window, I stared at the cold cobbled land. I have wanted to see the northern regions since I was very young, when I fell for *Manka the Sky Gypsy* by BB, about a pink-footed goose which migrated to and from Spitzbergen. The high north is a frigid paradise in BB's descriptions: cliffs of birds, tundra, snow hares and Arctic foxes. Then Alistair MacLean's *Ice Station Zebra* gripped me; I read him deep into the night, imagining the scream of the polar winds and the unseen tracks of nuclear submarines beneath the ice cap. Later came Barry Lopez's *Arctic Dreams*, and last year I was asked to review *A Farewell to Ice* by Peter Wadhams, which engrossed and terrified me.

From Wadhams, one of the world's leading authorities on sea ice, I learned that ice is extraordinary stuff, like water with twists. A 'puckered honeycomb' of oxygen and hydrogen atoms, ice is highly mutable in different states because the length of the hydrogen bonds in its molecules varies. Ice exists near absolute zero, the lowest temperature theoretically possible. Recent research suggests it may have entirely covered the planet three times, making 'snowball earths'. Ice coats space dust, giving stars their twinkle. Life may have originated in this shining matter, according to the astronomer Fred Hoyle. Sea ice functions as earth's air- and water-conditioning system, our thermostat, and we know that it is melting at an unprecedented rate. But the kind Wadhams worries about most covers the Arctic seabed, permafrost from the last ice age. Losing this will release huge methane plumes. Methane is twenty-three times more effective in raising global temperatures than carbon dioxide. Wadhams and colleagues have modelled different dates for methane release. If humanity continues to warm the world as we are now, Wadhams believes catastrophic methane plumes will erupt as soon as 2035. The worst floods, fires, droughts and storms we have seen will be as nothing in comparison to what Africa, Asia and the Americas are likely to experience in the case of 'runaway warming' caused by massive methane release. Millions would die, low-lying areas would be inundated and survivors would live in a patchy post-apocalypse. Europe's current refugee crisis would be dwarfed.

Travelling the Bay of Bothnia and talking to people who spend half their lives working on it should give me a rare perspective on sea ice. If Wadhams is right, we are going to need to know much more about this vital crystal.

Helsinki's Saturday-morning traffic was a straggle of democratically filthy vehicles spattering through slush into a low-rise city. The buildings were stoical in expression, as though they had endured many winters without great loss of face. Patches of grass were wilted yellow-green, scalded by snow. My hotel, the Vaakuna, was built for the 1952 Olympics, its lobby ringed with wooden thrones like a conference chamber for elves, the swish and flash of the international hospitality industry blissfully absent. Bags dumped, out into Helsinki I went, watched over by four severe and long-haired granite giants, each grasping a globe lamp. They guard the central railway station, its arches a looping entrance to an art nouveau otherworld. The curving mass of the edifice speaks of formidable self-assertion; the giants, magnificently straight-backed, look like warrior-priests. They were created in 1911, during the last years of Russian hegemony. Behind us is the world, their bearing suggests, but we gaze on Finland.

Under the gaze of the lamp-bearers the pedestrians were phlegmatic, navigating the slush and ice. There was a doughtiness about the crowds; they dressed in flat blues and browns, all practicality. Helsinki feels like a common-sense sort of city until you try to cross the street. Civic-mindedness becomes eccentricity as knots of people stand beside empty roads in the shivering cold, waiting for the crossing signals. It would be open rebellion to step off the kerb alone. Of their national character I had gleaned that Finns are law-abiding, punctual and given to introducing themselves by saying their names while shaking hands rather than before or after contact is made.

Two Irishmen passed. One urgently demanded of his friend, 'What the *hell* is up with that language?'

Finnish chirrups, rattles and croons like a collision between Chinese and Greek. While Swedes and Norwegians understand one another, they do not understand Finns. Though Finnish descends from Proto-Uralic, which came out of the Urals around seven thousand years ago, Finnish and Russian have no common root. It being a good idea to imagine difficult travel situations before they arise, my preparations for this mission have involved envisaging standing on the deck of an icebreaker in minus twenty Celsius and utter darkness, reciting, 'Poo-hoo-koa koo-kaan tael-lae ayng-lahn-tia?'

If anyone there does speak English, this will be their cue.

The paving stones of Helsinki are heavy granite slabs; there is an echo of the old Russian Grand Duchy in their might and heft. From 1809, when Russia relieved Sweden of Finland, until independence in 1917, these roads were thronged with travellers to and from St Petersburg. The leisured classes of that city came here to holiday (the only way of going abroad, with foreign travel banned), while Alexander II, known to the Finns as the Good Tsar, effectively founded modern Finland. What had been a collection of Swedish-ruled provinces became a single autonomous nation governed by a Finnish senate which made representations to the tsar, largely independent of the Russian authorities. In order to weaken Sweden's hold over her former possession Alexander championed Finnish, ending the dominance of Swedish. He allowed the introduction of a Finnish currency, the markka, and promoted economic reform and railway construction, knitting the Grand Duchy to the imperial centre. The stitching has never quite been unpicked. Russia's tottering economy has contributed to the longest recession in Finland since the war. As yet the Finns are weathering it. 'Well-being high, economy weak' is the verdict of the Organisation for Economic Cooperation and Development.

South towards the sea art nouveau rises again in terraces; *Jugendstil* the Finns term it, using the German for 'youth style'. The houses in their yellows, pinks and blues seem venerable and youthful at once, like pensioners in carnival gear. The terraces of Belgravia and the mansions of the sixteenth arrondissement of Paris are overblown compared to these pleasing and pretty streets, the houses decked in joyful colours, their bay windows, turrets, small spires and bas-reliefs speaking of a lightness and playfulness of wealth. Contrary tensions of East and West flicker in the atmosphere and architecture: there are Gothic echoes of Prague in some of the mansion flats; in the Liberty style of others, and in the dock cranes and quays, the intertwining of sea and city, there is something of Trieste. There was a lovely in-betweenness in the city that Saturday afternoon, as a pallid sun broke out, dog-walkers appeared, and at the seafront a glittering soup of ice slush hushed against the shore.

The traveller is obliged to have a sauna in Finland. As a Finn you take your first before you are six months old. On average the population steams and sweats itself every ten days. I found one by the sea but it was not accepting walk-ins. The democracy of Finnish sauna culture means that you are not refused entry because you have not reserved a place, but on the practical grounds that you have not booked space in the wardrobes for boots and coats. I deferred my steaming to the ship (all Finnish icebreakers have saunas) and feasted in the health centre restaurant on fish soup, black bread and reindeer shin. Beyond the windows cruise ships and ferries made for Estonia, Sweden and Russia. At other tables glossy women and neat men ate slowly, an air of deep and gentle satisfaction in the room. Reindeer is delicious, tanged and redolent of berries and heathers. From here, looking south, with Europe and the world somewhere below the horizon, it felt as though we were looking on, almost looking down, as though the northern rim afforded a privileged view. They looked future-proofed, those Finns. The fires and famines will not reach them.

I thought about how my heroines and heroes would approach the rest of the evening. Jan Morris would wander the streets. Her first essay on Helsinki dances with the relief of leaving the Soviet Union of the 1950s. Of the local citizenry she said, 'They are a people that nobody in the world, not even the heart-throb marching progressive, could possibly feel sorry for. They are as tough as nails, and twice as spiky.' On a return journey thirty years later she declared Finland the 'Lucky Country'. Michael Jacobs would have followed a tip to a dive bar, and made friends over food and drink. Norman Lewis would have sidled in and out of Helsinki without anyone noticing him, and missed nothing.

My wanderings have taught me that first you should eat as well as you can afford; whatever follows will be the better for it. Then I tend to lope about hopefully, on the lookout for good talkers. The Finns are going to test this strategy because they define themselves as taciturn introverts, though they have apparently changed much since the explorer and composer Giuseppe Acerbi published his *Travels through Sweden, Lapland and Finland* in 1798. 'The people have a gloomy and ferocious deportment,' he wrote.

'The young of both sexes remain in the company of each other without the least of that playful gaiety which is so becoming in their years. I never once observed a young man direct a smile of compliance towards a young woman …'

Acerbi would have been dazzled by the boisterous crowds in Helsinki on Saturday night and ascribed their metamorphosis to drink. Women downed pints of lager, and here and there men sat alone, some smiling, quietly and decisively smashed. The main action on the streets seemed to be negotiation with bouncers. Stolid imperturbable men in black held long conversations with swaying hopefuls, a notable lack of anxiety or aggression on either side. Given that Finnish education is free to doctorate level it is quite possible they all had PhDs.

In the end I deferred exploring to Oulu and the north the next day. In truth I was listless with the land. I longed for the day after tomorrow, and the ice, and the ship. This transition time is particular and isolated, as you remember who you are alone and fit yourself around the shape of the missing pieces of you, your family. I wished they were with me, making a mess of a table, charging into Finnish legs, marvelling at the Wi-Fi, whingeing, rowing, laughing.

* * *

Morning brought a darker Helsinki, smearing rain falling on a city still prey to Russian moods. Outside the museum a bronze horseman and his mount overlooked the traffic, the animal alert as if it had seen some threat, the rider casting a wider gaze as if he looked out on a vista. On the plinth the legend MANNERHEIM suggested no other words were necessary.

A Swedish-speaking Finn of an aristocratic family, Lieutenant General Carl Gustaf Mannerheim had thirty years' service in the Russian army behind him when he fled the Bolshevik revolution in 1917, returning to Finland, which declared independence in December of that year. A power vacuum, food shortages, the disbanding of the gendarmerie and the revolution beyond the Russian border made a crisis of class division. Socialist ideals and the inspiration of the Bolsheviks led urban and rural labourers to form the Red Guards and set up a revolutionary government in Helsinki. The government declared the bourgeois Civil Guard the army of the state and withdrew to Vaasa on the Bothnian coast, splitting the country between the largely White-held north and the Red industrial south. Appointed commander of the White forces, Mannerheim was able to deploy the Jäger Battalion, a thousand Finns who had volunteered to fight for Germany in the Great War, accompanied by ten thousand German soldiers sent by the kaiser to form another front against Russia.

The White Devil, the Reds called Mannerheim for his brutal victory in the battle for Tampere, the major industrial city of the south. Two thousand Reds were killed in the fighting and ten thousand captured, many dying in captivity of disease and starvation. The Red terror in the civil war killed over fifteen hundred Whites; it took decades for the scale of the reciprocal White terror to emerge. Ten thousand Reds were summarily executed and eighty thousand interned in camps, where an estimated twelve and a half thousand died of hunger and Spanish flu. The end of the war in 1918 drove many Reds to emigrate; thousands crossed the border into Russia, where they would eventually face Stalin's purges.

If his initial intervention in Finland's history was fearsome, Mannerheim's subsequent feats were extraordinary. He managed to distance Finland from the kaiser's Germany in the eyes of the victorious Allies, established the nation as an independent state and brought the Swedish-speaking Åland Islands (at the mouth of the Gulf of Bothnia) under Helsinki's control – one of the few achievements of the League of Nations. In 1919 Mannerheim rejected an attempt by hardline Whites to install him as a dictator. Serving as regent for six months, he persuaded the Allies that Finland should receive grain shipments, thereby saving the nation from famine. Having lost the election for first president of Finland, Mannerheim devoted himself to child welfare, travel and arguing for the strengthening of the Finnish armed forces. By the late 1930s he was pointing to the threat from the east and begging for resources to build up the army or leave to retire. Neither were forthcoming. He stepped down from an advisory post to the army aged seventy-two.

Two days into his retirement the Soviet Union shelled the border and bombed Helsinki. Mannerheim was immediately made commander-in-chief of the armed forces of a country suddenly united. His total forces numbered less than a third of the million Soviet soldiers who now attacked Finland on multiple fronts. Lacking men, material and preparedness, Finland should have been overrun in weeks. The means and manner of their resistance made Finland and Mannerheim famous, along with a Finnish word, *sisu*, which summed up the attitude of the defenders.

* * *

No one looked up at Mannerheim that grizzly day. On my way out of the city, on the airport bus, I watched the cloud break to the north-west. In a high gap appeared a gold-scaled chalcedony blue like a promise of adventure. At the departure gate my fellow travellers for Oulu were notably well covered, bulked out in woollens and coats. We landed in darkness. Beyond the windows, under the airport lights, the world was suddenly white.

CHAPTER 3

Oulu

S NOW! I had forgotten the joy of it, the amazement and delight of it, the all-changing miracle of its deepening. The cold was abrupt and thrilling, like icy hands fishing for your ribs. With three Austrian men I engaged a taxi to the Lapland hotel, which aspired to be in Lapland clearly, though Oulu is actually in Ostrobothnia. Finland's west coast retains its Swedish name, 'east bay', or 'eastern bottom' (lowlands). Names have become divorced from logic, remarrying practicality and commerce. We took off along a double strip of ice, clouds of snow blooming behind the car. On studded tyres we skidded like a boat onto the motorway. The driver's thick cap and thick glasses made him look like a half-blind fisherman. He accelerated to ninety kilometres an hour, relaxed. The Austrians were impressed.

'I like Finland, it is very laid-back,' said their leader, hanging on to a strap just in case. 'We are in gems and crystals! We are working for Swarovski. We are here meeting VTT.'

VTT, the state-owned Finnish technical research company, is pioneering 5G in Oulu. The fifth generation of wireless technology will allow faster Internet speeds, enabling 'beautiful variables', the Austrian said. 'One day your ring will monitor your health, or your brooch will tell you to go to a doctor.'

Highly skilled technicians have been coming to Finland for a long time thanks to Nokia, a Finnish company making paper when Finland was still a Grand Duchy, which went on to lead the world in mobile phones during the period of their exponential growth. Between 1992 and 2000 Nokia's phenomenal rise carried Finland with it. At the turn of the millennium, Nokia, with a staggering 41 per cent of the world mobile phone market, accounted for 4 per cent of Finland's GDP and a fifth of Finnish exports. Its profits were not buried offshore: Nokia rescued Finland from the banking crisis and recession of the early nineties with huge tax revenues and twenty thousand jobs. The country was able to make investments in education and technology that transformed it. When

Nokia fell, deposed by the rise of smartphones, its legacies of entrepreneurship, technology start-ups and a highly employable workforce meant Finland still prospered. If Mannerheim founded Finland's first century, its second is being built on the back of Nokia.

'Beautiful variables' was so pleasing I adopted it as my expedition motto. At the hotel we checked in, the Austrians turned in, and I set out into the peace and wide silence of the night, determined to grasp something of Finland and snow-test this ridiculously orange coat.

The receptionist was adamant: the place to go at that hour was in the centre and it did delicious burgers. I emerged from the snow into a small wooden cabin of a place decorated with benevolent graffiti.

LILLUHHEET WAS HERE declared a loopy hand. Double consonants are a particular trick of Finnish – you spin them out with a relishing stutter-pause.

'What sauce would you like?'

'What have you got?'

'We have nine types of mayonnaise and twenty-six kinds of beer.'

One should have little truck with burgers, I know, but when in Oulu ... The burger arrived and multiple mayonnaises made dreadful sense. Ninety sauces could not have improved the monster, suppurating sugar and salt. The locals adored them. At midnight customers were still coming in. 'After Finland, the worst food in the world,' Jacques Chirac said of British cuisine. 'To be endured,' said Silvio Berlusconi of Finland's. The British might have relished these burgers after gallons of drink, but the Finns here were apparently sober. It rather changed the weight of the proverb. 'The brave eat the soup, the timid die of hunger' may not be about courage but cookery.

There was no late-night feel in the cafe and I wondered, if half the year is basically darkness and the other half always light, if you can work on your phone via 5G any time, anywhere, and if there is always somewhere open, then had not the clock lost some of its grip on the psyche? There seemed a universal absence of rush. It was the weekend, but still I had seen no taut faces. Have the Finns found a loophole in the tyranny of long demands and short time?

At the bar up the street I ordered a nightcap.

'Good choice,' said a rich American voice thoughtfully.

* * *

Erick was famous, you could see it immediately; some combination of charisma and the way light liked him. 'I'm an actor,' he confessed, 'And I work here.' He had the policeman's trick of quick listening, prompting you to talk. His own story came out rapidly. After 'a period in the military' he became a private investigator in Albany, New York State. He married a Finn, a literature specialist whose work brought them here. They were divorced now. Erick had stayed in Finland to be near his daughter.

With sudden animation he spoke of his investigative work, of finding a man in days who had been on the run for months.

'The guy who hired me said, "How did you do that? *How did you do that?*" He wanted to make me a partner.'

The triumph subsided wistfully. Although he had good Finnish, Erick lacked the deeper local knowledge and the contacts which would allow him to practise investigating here. Instead of tracking down targets he scanned the bar. Men shook his hand and women hugged him as he asked how they were.

A blonde woman with a lurching gaze lamented her loss of Finnish. 'Been in fucking Portugal all these fucking years and now my language is gone fuck.'

'I told you not to go,' Erick said.

A swaying woman emerged from the shadows and spoke to Erick in what sounded like cuckoo calls played backwards, a dialect blend of alcohol, affection and Finnish. He made sure she knew where she was going and was accompanied.

'You know everyone!'

'Oh yeah. We did that British musical, *The Full Monty*?'

'Did you do the *full* Monty?'

'Every night. In Finnish. For weeks.'

'What was that like?'

'We were swamped,' he said, making comical saucers of his eyes.

When the bar shut, Erick led me to 45, which stayed open into the small hours. There was live music downstairs and bars above, and very soon Erick was swamped again and I was talking to a mysterious Swede about Russia and submarines. He was an intense young man, friendly, forward-bent like a heron, given to covering his mouth with his hand and looking you hard in the eye.

'Where are the Finnish submarines?' he asked.

'You tell me!'

'Finland is not allowed any. The Paris treaty, 1947. But Finns were expert submarine builders. They built the U-boats!'

The prototypes for the Nazi U-boat fleet were constructed here, funded by Germany as the country sought to dodge the stipulations of the Treaty of Versailles.

'Perhaps Finland is the hidden knife in Nato's coat!' he said.

The Russians are alert to the notion. 'Nato would have no qualms about fighting Russia down to the last Finnish soldier,' Vladimir Putin told a press conference in Finland last year. The Finnish press reported that the line was delivered with a smirk. Russia has re-opened an abandoned military base on the Kola peninsula, forty miles from the border. Mobile anti-aircraft missile systems have been moved up to the Finnish frontier and nuclear missiles stationed in Kaliningrad. To the north Russia has renovated and constructed a string of military bases on Franz Josef Land, Novaya Zemlya, Northern Island and the New Siberian Islands. By 2018 it plans nine bases with airstrips in the Arctic. The high north is suddenly a contested place. Sweden has just reintroduced conscription, while in Finland all males turning eighteen are called up for military service, with 70 per cent completing it. (The rest do longer civilian service, with a stalwart fifty individuals a year sent to prison for conscientious objection.)

Soon we were picking our way across the town through the snow, ending up in someone's flat for a continuation party, and then the sky greyed through the windows and Oulu emerged, deep in crystals, the dawn glowing with a strange luminescence, light both soft and bright kindled between snow and sky.

As I took my leave, Erick was relaxing on the floor, cradled by his sister-in-law. I had been told about Finnish benefits (good) and rents (high), Russians (enigmatic), and Erick had imparted a ruse by which you might serve divorce papers on a runaway American husband: find out where he works and gain entry by claiming to be his cousin – if both of you are black no one will question you until you slap the papers on him. I had been introduced to Finnish laws (humane) and judges (enlightened), the comfort and splendour of Oulu flats (considerable), and Finnish hospitality (near paralysing).

A musician and his friend outlined Finnish feelings about their neighbours.

'So you like the Danes?'

'Umm yeah …' they equivocated, wobbling flat palms in the air.

'The Norwegians?'

'The Norwegians are OK.'

'The Swedes?'

'Nooo!' they chorused.

'What's wrong with the Swedes?'

'Ooh ... everything! No ... not really ...'

'Well ...'

'They did invade us a lot.'

Sweden, Christian and powerful, invaded the pagan Finnish wilds in a series of crusades, taking the south-west corner in 1248 and expanding across the territory, dominating the south-west by 1323, gaining the lot by 1617 and holding most of it until the Finnish War of 1808. In that year Sweden and Russia fought over Finland, as opposed to fighting in Finland, which they did regularly, notably in 1590 (the Russo-Swedish War) and again from 1700 to 1720 (the Great Northern War).

Victorious, finally, in 1808, Russia controlled the Grand Duchy of Finland until 1917. Thus the ruling class of Finland were Swedes for the best part of seven centuries – longer, if you credit medieval Swedish chron-iclers who claim the First Crusade of 1248 was actually the Second, the sequel to an original crusade which did or did not take place around 1150. There is no written or archaeological evidence for this expedition, but it does make a fine justification for a 'successor' a century later.

Farewells made, I stepped out into the early light, having taken a bearing on the spire of the cathedral, built by Finns under Russian rule and attached to an eighteenth-century church named after the wife of a Swedish king.

CHAPTER 4

Otso

THE TAXI curves out of Oulou, takes a long dog-leg around the port and approaches a barrier. At the word '*Otso!*' the lady on watch waves us through. We slither over frozen ground to the end of a long quay.

Icebreaker *Otso* rises above black water and ice patches, snow jumbling in the wind. The ship looks like a sawn-off ferry, her hull planed down, low and rolling, her superstructure bulked up. A hundred metres long and forty metres high, seven thousand tonnes of her tower above the quay, her harbour generators humming and roaring, air intakes rushing. She is a snub blue-and-white machine, carrying her orange lifeboats high up on each side like tiny water wings. Her master comes down the gangway.

Teemu Alstela is a burly man, young for a captain and blond-bearded, the golden spines of his moustache a jutting overhang, a hairy spindling that must function as insulation. His eyes are a snow-pale shade of grey I have not seen before, and he seems amused. I think it may be my coat. His is a slow and forgiving scrutiny. I have been foisted on him by Arctia, the state-owned company responsible for keeping Finland's sea trade running through the ice. I will mean work and answering questions, but perhaps diversion too, says his hopeful smile.

'Welcome, welcome! I am Tem.'

He leads me aboard. *Otso* is slipper-shaped, a low stern rising and flaring to a wide bow. In the centre the raked white pyramid of her superstructure, smartly striped with Finnish blue, rises ten storeys above the waterline. Stickled with ladders, gantries and pipes, she feels tough and competent, smelling of steel, refuse and diesel. Entry is via a small hatchway with a high sill. The corridors are narrow and warm, scented with coffee and cooking – spicy chicken? She seems well worn rather than hard-driven, scrubbed and brushed; like all of the Finland I have seen, she is impeccably clean.

'We have this present for you.' Tem hands over a splendid white hard hat with HORATIO IB OTSO ARCTIA

ICEBREAKING labelled across the peak. 'Ice and things can fall off from above, so please wear this when you are outside.'

The solicitous concern and Tem's soft manner are disarming. A collection of men, engineers, are sprawled in the engine control room. We all say 'Hei!' This is a refreshingly simple communication, the only such example in Finnish.

Greeting the men and being looked over by them is like entering a working men's club. Icebreaker crews become closely associated with one or two ships, returning to their main vessel and each other repeatedly. The febrile atmosphere you detect on some ships when new crew join is absent here. I feel like a new boy starting school in the middle of term.

'Now we will see if we get stuck!' Tem says almost hopefully, opening a small lift. We go four decks up and climb a stair to the bridge. In the middle in front of the windows is a control position, complete with a Morse code key, a small steering wheel and throttles. On the port wing is a second set of engine controls, and on the starboard side is an amazing chair mounted on rails in the deck, in front of the third steering position, the one they generally use. The wing positions are housed in octagonal turrets, thickly glassed in, which stick out from either side of the bridge. Steering from here, the helmsman can see behind and beside *Otso* as clearly as he can ahead. Being able to judge what is happening all around an icebreaker is crucial, I will learn. They work in dangerous proximity to other ships.

The bridge is a full orchestra of technology. Here are radar screens, computers, throttles, rudder controls, bow thruster and the controls for the 'bubbler', which pumps air out of the sides of the ship below the waterline, reducing friction with the ice. At the rear of the bridge a chart table is surrounded by screens, radar displays, at least six radios, three satellite links, displays showing weather, ice, other ships and the heeling tank, echo sounder, searchlight controls, schematics for engines and ballast, dials showing power outputs, switchboards, telex printers, Inmarsat printer . . . There must be thirty screens.

'Vill-ay, first officer,' says a large young man as I bungle the simultaneous handshake and introduction protocol. Ville's face is a collection of curves, like a baby ogre. His hair is clipped short, and he trims his beard into a chin-strap. He is wearing a grey tracksuit and sandals. Everyone is dressed for slouching in front of the TV. Ville has the air of a shy man with much to do.

'Sampo,' says a smiling man with a suave air, clothed in charcoal colours, smarter than Ville's rig. Sampo is the second officer – younger than Ville, I think, but it is hard to tell. He is an ageless, unlined man, his greying hair an immaculate swoop and his manner not at all shy. 'If you come with me ...' He has a rapid and rapidly assessing quality about him and his English is perfect. Down we go to the main deck, and over to the seaward side.

'This is your lifeboat, starboard. If you hear the alarm you come here.'

We agree that lifeboats are horrible, dangerous things, and I compliment him on his ship.

'Only a bit of rust,' he says, looking at a spatter of flaked patches on the steel. 'The Bay of Bothnia is hardly salty at all, about 0.2 per cent.'

We go up and down stairs rapidly, along corridors, up again, down again.

'In here ... we eat – breakfast five thirty, lunch at eleven thirty, dinner at five thirty. Down here is the gym. Here is the sauna. Two saunas, one for officers, one for crew. The laundry is in here. We have a conference room but we don't use it. Lounge ...'

My cabin is spacious, with a couch and desk, a bunk and a shower. The windows are double-glazed, thick plastic on the inside, glass on the outside. There are drawers with things in them, and trays and shelves and all manner of small treasures and documents others have left.

Forward lines let go, stern lines let go, spring lines let go. No pilot, for all the navigating officers hold pilotage licences, and no tug. *Otso* is under Tem's fingertips as he makes tiny adjustments on throttles and bow thruster, turns the dial controlling the two rudders and moves us slowly, slowly away from the berth. He will not handle the ship again until we return to port.

'Why does the captain do this bit?'

'Kind of ... tradition. Yes. This is when you can hit things with everyone watching!'

Our only audience, dock workers in bright green jackets, hurry away as soon as the lines are cast off. Diggers and trucks are working a wasteland of dirty snow, while a refinery adds steam to a steam-coloured sky. In sheened black water ice floats in shattered fragments. The only motion outside is three hooded crows, heading in a straggle for an island through huge stillness. You can see silence here. The atmosphere on the bridge is hushed, almost reverent, as we depart at a stately pace towards the frozen sea.

From the bridge we stare at a sea without tides, without waves, almost without salt and now, to the eye, without water. We run into a skin of ridged ice, black-lined by the wind where the snow has blown away. Channel buoys stand rigid, frozen in place. A dark nodule off the port bow is a seal like a fat semi-colon; flapping away to the south, neck thrust forward between enormous wings, is a sea eagle, intent as an assassin. There is excitement on the bridge at the sight of the creatures, a chatter of Finnish and a grabbing of binoculars. 'Icebreakers used to hunt seals!' Ville says.

The ice stretches to opaque horizons. As the lines of the forests fall away behind us, all bearings seem lost. Our black track rocking with shards is the only distinction, as if we are the tip of a pencil trailing a line into empty space.

Now Tem is on the phone he carries in a thigh pocket, coordinating the other icebreakers. He has half a dozen to assign, scattered up and down the gulf.

'One is being repaired, so they thought it was a good idea to hire another from Sweden. He's asking for work,' Sampo says.

On a whiteboard there are ships' names, port names and times, indicating whether the vessels are leaving or arriving, and noting where we will find them. This is our to-do list, Sampo explains.

'The ice is thickest at the edges of the bay, so we lead them in or out, but it depends where the ice is and where they get stuck. The rule of thumb in icebreaking is everything changes all the time.'

My assumptions about icebreaking were wrong. I had imagined we would be trundling up and down the Bay of Bothnia, cracking open the shipping channels – known as fairways – keeping them ice-free so that the trade upon which Finland relies might continue to flow through the winter. In fact, a newly broken fairway might remain passable for hours, but it is just as likely the ice will close up again in minutes, even seconds. Every ship hoping to cross the Bay of Bothnia will need an icebreaker, certainly near the ports and possibly out at sea as well. I had supposed container ships carrying food and goods would be our main customers, but the list shows that few are transporting containers; bulk carriers, ore carriers, colliers and chemical tankers will be our business. Working south-wards from the bay's most northerly point there are six main ports –Tornio, Kemi, Oulu, Raahe, Rajha and

Kokkola, all frozen in – but Tem cannot just assign one icebreaker to each port, because out in the gulf is the drift ice, trapping ships on their way to or from Sweden and the Baltic.

'For some reason no one else wants to do this coordinating-captain job,' Tem says slowly, grinning, 'I always do it. And when it all goes wrong, we fix it.'

'How much does an icebreaker cost?' I ask Sampo.

'About twenty thousand euros per day, if you want to hire us.'

'Do you charge the ships for help?'

'They pay a fairway tax – that includes us.'

Beyond the bridge screens we can see the fairway, a channel marked with buoys, safe for navigation in this shallow sea. Further from shore where the buoys give out, the safe channel is marked on electronic and paper charts. We can see what appears to be the fairway in the broken and rubbled track left by previous ships, but this is misleading, Tem says.

'The ice is always moving. If you only follow the track it can take you away, and the bay is very shallow. Every year this happens.'

'Where are we going, Captain?'

'We are going to Raahe. We have some ships there.'
Tem loves the sounds of Finnish words. 'Raahe' is spoken
with a roll on the 'r' and a skip in the middle: 'Rror-hey'.

'How far is it?'

'Ah I don't think in distance! Only in time. We will
be there in four hours.'

I will learn that there are no distances in the Bay of
Bothnia. There are speeds of wind and speeds of ice
drift. There are hours of dark, hours of light and hours
of twilight. There are ships' waiting times and our
expected times of arrival. But distance is nothing here.
Distance is only the time it takes for us to cross a floe,
to forge through a lead, to break into the next white
field. Sometimes cracks shoot ahead of us across the
pack, black lines in long curly breaks, as though the ice
fractures along preordained faults. Sometimes it seems
all our transits are fated, as the helmsman stares ahead
and the engines beat and the mist gathers or falls back,
and the light brightens or dims and the ice thins and
thickens. We will arrive, we will break and turn and
break again.

Outside I go, diligently suited and helmeted, eyes
streaming at the cold. Expose a hand for thirty seconds
and you can feel the blood being squeezed out of your

fingers. There is no sensation of water motion at all, only the grating, barrelling cacophony of the hull crashing through the ice. Our rolling collision sounds like a giant steel wheelbarrow being dragged upside down over a stony yard. The deck rumbles and bobbles underfoot. An icebreaker works by thrusting the curving weight of its bow up onto the pack, the drive of the engines and the weight of the ship pushing it forward and down. Over ice like this, twenty centimetres thick, you feel no lateral or vertical movement. Instead there is a constant shuddering, as though the ship is tearing herself over a reef.

To the south-west is a stain of sunset between the ice and sky, a cold pink blush. The ice is slightly brighter than the air; together they seem to collect light and focus it on the ship, so that her surfaces, her rusts and paint-work, her rails and sills, her winches and ropes glow slightly, every detail in definition.

'Sheeiw, but it's *cold*!' I gasp, back on the bridge.

Sampo laughs. 'Minus ten. In minus twenty you can actually see the water freeze, really fast, just – *skoosh!*' He throws a gesture across the bay, casting a spell. 'And you know it's minus twenty when your nose squeezes up. It kind of contracts.'

I lean against the windows, which go floor to ceiling, armoured glass three centimetres thick. Below us the solidified sea is hypnotic, the cracking white breaking with black lines, leaving peat-coloured water in our wake.

'What kind of ice is this?'

'This is compacted ice. It's been broken and frozen together. When we get to consolidated ice, the heavy stuff? That can double or triple fuel consumption. We'll get through a hundred tonnes of fuel in twenty-four hours. When you think an average family house in Finland might need one and half tonnes for a whole year ... You can just leave your car running if you're icebreaking!'

It emerges that Sampo has strong feelings about cars.

'I got a Silverado. I've been doing some building work on the house, and it's good for carrying stuff,' he says. If he could look sheepish he would, but Sampo was not made for embarrassment.

A Chevrolet Silverado is an absurd machine, over four tonnes of steel, bull-headed intimidation and giant wheels, achieving a laughable nineteen miles to the gallon. Most four-by-four drivers could curse Sampo as an environmental war criminal without feeling a twinge of hypocrisy. Thankfully we have *Otso*, her sisters and her charges, absolving the SUV drivers of Finland. And beyond Bothnia we have all the ships at sea today, expelling so much carbon dioxide that measured as a nation they constitute the seventh most polluting country on earth.

It takes me a while to stop calling Tem 'Captain'. Informality is a Finnish trait. When the USSR attacked the country in 1939 Soviet brigades were coldly hierarchical, controlled by officers and policed by commissars. The opposing Finnish units were often made up of men from the same region. They referred to their officers by name or nickname, authority a personal quality more than an institutional imposition. Dash, flexibility, improvisation and *sisu* underlay the fighting quality of the defenders. Finns do not boast about it, but holding off overwhelming Soviet forces and later defeating German units in Lapland gave the young country a foundation of tremendous pride and self-belief.

Sisu is the key. It has no single equivalent in English, but denotes a gritty, courageous and robust refusal to be beaten. Finnish soldiers invented the Molotov cocktail to attack Soviet tanks, aiming to souse the machines' air ducts with blazing petrol. (Eighty-seven women and five men produced over half a million of these weapons until their factory was destroyed. Finnish manufacturing pride led early bottles to be sealed with tops giving the factory's address.) They levered off Russian tank tracks with stakes and bars. They shot at the gunners' eye slits with pistols, the very definition of *sisu*.

'So this word *sisu*, Tem, does it mean a lot to you?'

'Yes. I suppose so. Well for me I think, *Chin on chest and head on to the next disappointment!*'

He laughs with the gaiety of a man whose head would never be allowed to slump and who must have known disappointments but not many.

The Swedish icebreaker *Frej* passes in the long twilight. Even in February the dimming time lasts and lingers, a heavy pewter, as if the sky weighs more than the frozen sea. We pass *Frej* in brash ice, a slushy mosaic which has formed, broken and been repacked by the wind. Her charge, an orange gas carrier, follows a hundred metres behind.

'The rule of thumb,' Sampo says – Sampo is very fond of rules of thumb – 'is that if the distance between the ships is such that the vessel you are leading is not in danger of crashing into you, she will get stuck. It's not so bad in a big fairway, but in the open sea you can find compacted ice like cement. You hit it, *wham*! You stop, and the ship behind you goes into you. All we can do is tell them to turn hard to starboard, but the gap is so narrow. Actually we have a big crack in the stern …'

Supper is pork, rice and salad, prepared by Ulla and Pentti. Ulla is a woman with a shy, sweet aspect and no English. I will seek her out after every meal and thank her, and each time she will duck and smile. Pentti is a hulking man in chef's trousers, his face grizzled, who smokes noisome cigars. He has labelled each dish with a note in English. SOUP, FISH. SOUP, VEGETABLE. PORK, MEAT. POTATOES. Tomorrow will be SALMON, FISH.

'The best is Jansson's Temptation,' says Tem. 'Fish and onions and potatoes.'

Pentti's painstaking labelling is not only for me. We have a second passenger aboard, Reidun, a Norwegian geophysicist. Reidun is a hero to the crew. Two years ago her company chartered *Otso* for a voyage to Greenland to make seismic surveys for the oil industry.

'We thought if you came back you could get us another voyage,' Sampo tells her.

'I wish I could,' Reidun says.

'You're not working now?'

'No. No, this is my holiday,' Reidun says. Her daughter is at university in Britain. Reidun works, climbs and yearns for travel. She and Sampo have a delightful friendship, as though he has adopted her as a kind of super-aunt. She is the only one on the ship who can still teach him tricks in the ship's databases. Her eyes are an astonishing blue, and she has a slightly unnerving way of holding your gaze in silence, as though you are a study subject. This trick provokes Tem to heavily comical sallies in which he claims he cannot do anything, does not know anything, does not really work and survives by lowering his chin to his chest and heading for the next disappointment. There is much reminiscence about their previous voyage.

'The North Atlantic was the stuff of dreams,' Sampo says. 'We came back through storms. When the waves were the height of the bridge I turned the searchlights off. Enough! I'd rather not see them!'

He has also been along the Northern Sea Route, which runs along the top of Russia, emerging in the Bering Strait.

'With two Russian icebreakers, nuclear-powered.'

'God, what a voyage! What was it like?'

'Pitch black for two weeks. You get into this black tube and after two weeks you pop out on the other side of the world. So far north there are a lot of time zones. You adjust your clock twice a day.'

CHAPTER 5

Silence

AFTER DINNER I join Pentti in the smoking room.
The smoking room is a steel box accessed from the
main deck, a stinking coffin decorated with *Playboy*
calendars dating back to 2010, each displaying a winter
month with all the days neatly crossed out.

'So this is the art gallery?'

'Yes.'

'Have you been a cook on ships for a long time?'

'All my life.'

'Would you ever cook on land?'

'No!'

'Why?'

'Why not?'

'What's it like cooking on a ship?'
'It's OK.'

He is very shy and it is not fair to interrogate him. Let him finish his cigar in peace. Try this guy instead.
'Hello! I'm Horatio.'
'Ey.'
'What's your name?'
Mumble – sounds like Jouni?
'May I ask what you do?'
'Ey?'
'What do you do?'
'Engineer.'
'Ah right! So, what did you do today?'
Pained look. Pause. 'Some little bit.'
'And what will you do tomorrow?'
Agonised look. Hand to head. 'I don't know.'

Right. I had expected this. Sometimes I will meet men who do not have much English, who are shy and who have a Finnish reserve which is reputed to out-reserve even the British version. This is a Finnish silence! They are famous. They come in different grades. There are relaxed silences, companionable, puzzled, contented, unhappy, charged and thoughtful silences, even lyrical silences.

I will join Jouni in a thoughtful silence. He stares at the steel bulkhead, a good move given the alternatives are Heather's bum or Kyra's boobs. The bulkhead is pale yellow. Painted like that or nicotined over? Practice, a Finnish silence is just a question of practice. I can do this. Jouni is rubbing his jaw as if he has toothache. We can do this. We are in heavier ice now, the ship grating and vibrating. Jouni has half of his cigarette left. He is greyed and lined by cigarettes as I will be if I do not quit. I am doing this wrong. I am eating his silence – we can both feel it. No, worse, I am listening to his silence. Of course! How can you hope to share a silence if one of you is eavesdropping on the other? Quickly, I must listen to my own silence. Crash, thump, scrape, gripe goes the ice against the hull, and then if I can hear mine, and he his, might we then begin to hear, to share – clash, clash, grate – something? This is hopeless. Something just whimpered. Was it Jouni? Was it me? The women on the wall are laughing.

'Bye! Have a good evening.'

'Unph,' says Jouni.

I want desperately to apologise.

* * *

On the bridge we study the ice map, a satellite picture of the whole Gulf of Bothnia. The gulf has the outline of a squeezed figure of eight. The ice chokes the Bay of Bothnia, the northern oval, where we are, but it tails off south of us in the Kvarken Strait, the pinched neck where Sweden and Finland are only fifty miles apart, which divides the bay from the Bothnian Sea.

'Up here below Kemi they are cutting this piece off,' Tem says, the cursor moving across the bottom of a huge comma of ice. An icebreaker is making multiple passes along it, hoping the wind will move it west.

'Look at the long-term ice trend,' he says, bringing up a graph. 'From 1965 to 1986 most of the gulf was covered at this time of year.' Around the north and east coasts tonight there is a fat rind of 'fast ice', sheets that are attached to the land, and a thicker swelling of drift ice in the middle. The southern gulf is largely clear.

'This would be so nice!' Tem says wistfully, indicating the old seasonal average. 'We need a high pressure over Murmansk.' He points to the Russian port on the White Sea, far to the north-east. 'Then you get nuclear winter in Bothnia! Not rain. The low pressures are coming too far north. Everything goes OK as long as the Brits get the rain. I think it's Brexit. They are going to leave the

EU, and they don't want the rain any more so they send it here.'

At midnight we are parked in what looks like tundra, snow on ice shining in the searchlight beams. Our lights are a blazing array fore and aft, two white arms reaching out ahead of us, while a bank of smaller lamps creates a wobbly lens of light around the ship. We are a space station, a tent of light and power hovering until our charge comes out of Raahe, a small bulk carrier. She appears, and now the engines scream, Sampo deploying all four as we set off through consolidated brash ice, a packed jumble, wind broken and wind reformed. The coaster is close behind in our black wake, small and vulnerable, following us like an eerily obedient child. We turn her loose at the edge of the pack and steam back into thick ice. Sampo brings us to the most gentle, inching stop. Our speed through the water shows zero but the instruments still display a speed over ground as *Otso* drifts with the ice.

'You aren't going to anchor?'

'No, no, never. If you put the anchor down the ice won't give it back! We just park in the ice. It's moving at zero point three knots,' he says, 'So a mile every three hours. Should be fine.'

* * *

Still wakeful, I poke around my cabin. Time has paused here, leaving a cassette player built into a shelf and relics in the drawers. Here is a cup of Norwegian krone, holes punched through their centres, on top of a copy of *Newsweek* from 1995 – will Michael Jordan return to basketball? Underneath is a *National Geographic* from April 1979. The big question of that spring edition was WHAT ABOUT NUCLEAR ENERGY? There are advertisements for brown BMWs, Rolex watches and Beechcraft aeroplanes; there is a long feature on Old Prague, a city behind the Iron Curtain which the magazine treats as a lost world. The lead story comes from east Africa. Mary Leakey writes about her discovery and excavation of the Laetoli footprints, a set of bipedal tracks made by three of our ancestors around 3.6 million years ago in what is now Tanzania. My sense of time totters. From feeling old – I remember those antique BMWs, just – I am now too recently born and too soon dead to register on a timeline which would also show our forebears. *Otso*'s keel would have been riding where the top of her mast is now if she had been here when that little group left their footprints. There was no ice cap in the northern hemisphere. Sea levels were twenty-five metres higher than they are tonight. It was the Pliocene period, when global temperatures were two to four degrees higher than pre-industrial modern averages – 'In fact conditions were rather like those we are heading into as we modify our own climate,' Peter Wadhams writes in his *Farewell to Ice*. Agriculture would not have worked for the Laetoli hominids, who lived in downpours and heatwaves, but during the Pliocene earth's atmosphere cooled as the planet entered a series of ice ages separated by tens of thousands of years, the modern cycle.

We are a spaceship submerged under the ghost of a Pliocene sea at an echo-junction of climatic change points, our earth warming as theirs cooled. In a few decades there will again be no ice here; *Otso*'s descendants will be in the high north, defending Arctic oil rigs from fragments of the polar cap. Perhaps the most significant difference between us and the beings who made the footprints, across those millions of years, is that we know that change is coming, though we can only guess at its magnitude. I envy our ancestors their innocence and their solidarity. There has been speculation that the three sets of footprints were made by a family group going down to a waterhole, but there is no evidence for this. We do know that one of them was walking in the tracks of another, placing his or her feet in the leader's footprints. Was this a game? A ruse? Perhaps it is another echo. Perhaps we have always made tracks for our charges to follow. The wind has dropped outside. *Otso* is as silent as she can be, her ventilation humming.

CHAPTER 6

Ice and Albedo

D AWN IS a pale high blue, minus ten and colder with the windchill, ice showing in black scars where the wind has cleared it of snow. The pack is streaked with breaks, fractured lakes and linear pools called leads. The vocabulary of sea ice is a lovely mush of different languages. From Russian come *polynyas*, irregular lakes enclosed by ice, and *sastrugi*, sharp wind-formed ridges on floes, and *nilas*, a thin and bendy ice crust. From North America come bergy bits and growlers, different grades of iceberg; from Old High German and Swedish comes *firn*, a frozen crystallisation halfway between ice and snow.

Breakfast is turgid frankfurters and tasteless eggs. I vow not to get up for it again. Outside the cold makes your eyes cry. You inhale, and the frigid air makes your stomach lurch. We steam back to Raahe, in the early light a low shore, a sentry line of wind turbines and a steaming steel mill. Radios chirrup and growl in Finnish. Some of the voices sound as though they come from sea dogs, hard as rocks, surely bearded. Ville takes us close to the port, opening the channel, passing the little orange pilot boat, which looks bound in ice.

'When it freezes hard the pilots use an aluminium sledge to get to the ships,' he says. 'Three years ago one fell in.'

'Was he OK?'

'No, he died. Caught between the sledge and the ship. One of the crew was fishing at home last year, he heard a man fall through the ice. Screaming. They got him out, but brain damage.'

'How long do you have, if you go in?'

'In about five minutes you lose consciousness, in fifteen it's game over.'

'Have you ever been scared, Ville?'

'When I was young. Going from Holland to the UK there was a small hurricane in the North Sea. It was very rough. But I grew up on ships. My father was a chief engineer. I've been on ships since I was three years old.'

'Born to the sea!'

'It is hard sometimes, with my wife. But well paid and lots of holiday. And on icebreakers lots of steering! Every day is different.'

Tem says his wife understands. She was on ships too. 'We met on a ro-ro between Belgium and Middlesbrough. She was my senior officer.' ('Ro-ro' is short for roll-on, roll-off, most commonly referring to vehicle and passenger ferries.)

'How is it with your children, when you go away?'

'When they are little it is not so bad; when you go away they don't say anything. But now ... my son is seventeen, my daughter is ten. It is harder. They say why, why are you going away for three weeks? When are you coming back? I got home and my daughter wouldn't speak to me at all.'

He shakes his head. Then he brightens. 'I have a plan. In the half-term I am going to bring them aboard one at a time.'

'They will love that!'

'I hope so. But I am a little worried they will get bored. The Internet is quite slow. Perhaps I will bring some games. Xbox or something ...'

It is the only anxiety I have seen in Tem. The children of these icebreakers can lack for nothing financially. The cars and houses they talk about suggest high salaries. And when he is at home a father is soaked in time.

'I am the taxi driver,' Tem exclaims. He looks so happy at the thought. 'I do all that when I'm home! You want to go somewhere? You want Daddy to wait? OK! Let's go!'

'Supermarkets!' Ville exclaims. 'Being on the ship is no cooking, no washing-up and no supermarkets. I hate supermarkets.'

Perhaps Dad extends the house, buys and builds, like Sampo. When he is gone he is not far away and will be back soon. 'This is as close to seafaring as you can get without having to be always out there,' Sampo says. But 'not far away' and 'back soon' are poor currency as you offer them at the door, gently detaching yourself from your child's hugging arms.

We all send messages and love, hugs and photographs, and wait for anything back, any news. It is horrible to trade your presence for their security. All the officers and engineers have been on ships which took them away for weeks and months – they know it could be worse, it could always be worse. And the silence of wives and partners surrounds every conversation. The rhythm of the sailor's partner's life is single parent, spouse, single parent, spouse. Single parent: up at dawn, the school run, work, shopping, school run, cooking, children's bedtime, work, your bedtime, up at dawn – for half the year, in fragments. Nothing the men are doing out here is hard compared to that – highly skilled certainly, psychologically tough and increasingly draining as the voyage goes on (the navigating officers work six hours on, six hours off) but not hard.

The sea is ice-white to the horizon. Soft lavender and pink spreads where the sun rises into a white-blue sky.

'We are waiting for the ugliest ship in the Bay of Bothnia to come out,' Ville says. 'A barge and pusher.'

A barge and pusher looks like one craft, with a wheel-house at the back and a huge cargo hold at the front, but the two parts can be decoupled.

'What's she doing?'

'There's a big vessel in the gulf – there. See?'

The electronic chart shows *Arkadia* stationary to the south-west.

'*Arkadia* has coal from Poland. She's too deep to unload in the port so we lead the pusher out to her, and when she is loaded we bring her in. And we've got iron-ore carriers from Sweden coming down.'

A magenta light spreads across the horizon until the whole western sky glows. The sun now is orange in the east. Instead of warming, the temperature drops to minus twelve and I am nipping in and out of the bridge, trying to miss nothing of my first sub-Arctic sunrise. Luminous blues pool in our track. The ice is blue-sheened white. The forested shore looks like black moss around the rim of the ice. We steam down the fairway, broken ice now refrozen into thumping white cobbles. The noise and rumble are reassuring: we are working.

Reidun is discussing the ice map with Tem. There is rueful laughter at the diminished coverage and hope at the promise of colder winds and high pressure. The Polish coal Finland is importing this morning will kill the ice, of course. *Otso* would seem to be conniving in the destruction of her livelihood, but paradoxically the shrinking of the ice has increased the demand for icebreakers. In the Arctic glaciers are calving bergs of hard multi-year ice which thin or non-existent first-year ice now fails to contain. There will soon be many more ships running north of the Arctic Circle, in need of protection, rescue and cleared channels.

Now the pack is pinking as our shadow deepens to a dark and glowing petrol blue. The chief electrician comes up to fix a radio. Tem is fiddling with small cameras and mounts, and there is a happy chatter on the bridge, the sound of men with small fixable things to play with, equipment to assemble. You can feel their pleasure in occupation.

Wind-driven, the pack squeezes tight behind us, closing over the fairway almost as soon as we break it open. We keep the pusher barge within half a ship's length as we lead her out to *Arkadia*, the turbulence of our wake clearing a few metres of water in which she can move. The barge is a square-bowed brute, her bridge narrow and winged like a submarine's. Behind her comes the pilot boat carrying the crane operators who will work *Arkadia*'s derricks, transferring her coal into the barge. Fairy fires sparkle on the ice as the sun climbs. There are no birds flying, no seals to be seen, no planes overhead, and no movement anywhere but our convoy, shepherding coal buckets across ice like a blazing white moon. At the edge of the ice we pause, turn and escort the pilot boat back in. We turn again and set off into the pack. Now we park in the ice and let down the ladder. We are free until this evening and are going for a walk.

Can it possibly be safe? I have never stepped off a ship at sea before. Sampo is going to fly a drone. The quadcopter is as big as a suitcase. 'The ice is over twenty centimetres thick,' he says encouragingly, 'At forty you can drive a truck on it.'

'So you just … step off,' I tell myself, and do.

I can feel the sea underneath, I am sure. Something is not right, your feet insist. Is there some internal human gyroscope which senses that the sheet is moving with us on it? There is an apprehension of movement, something neither solid nor liquid under the snow. Scuffing the powder away reveals what looks like sinister black glass. Lifting your gaze to the horizon brings a giddiness of space; from down here the range of view seems infinite, a desert, an elation of light. Out of the ship's shade the glare is exhilarating, light flinging blue-gold out of the heavens, shadowless and ethereal. An elemental realm this, part desert, part sea, all its own. You feel dizzy, you feel like laughing, you feel like setting off for the horizon. There are no reference points but the ship.

Otso's blue hull rises out of broken slabs of green-white ice like jumbled tables. The slabs are topped with snow and underlaid with a layer of darker ice. In a Bothnian calm, molecules on the sea's surface freeze, forming crystalline lumps in the water. This is grease ice or *frazil*; we steamed through it coming out of Oulu, and it rubbles the edges of the pack and the fairway.

Without wind or waves the crystals join, becoming a thin sheet called *nilas*. *Nilas* divides the atmosphere from the water. Now congelation growth begins, with water molecules freezing on the bottom of the sheet. In the darker layer at the base of these slabs you can see a vertical shading, columns of crystals growing downwards, first-year ice which may thicken to a metre and a half up here, and to half a metre in the Antarctic. Because all the crystals in a first-year ice sheet are oriented in the same direction the sheet is mechanically weak, easily broken by an icebreaker's bow. The immediate question is how it reacts to compression forces, as I am standing on top of it.

We step gingerly around our vessel, which seems neither afloat nor aground, as if she had hovered down onto the surface. Her stern is an extended shelf, notched to accommodate the bows of a towed or pushed ship, padded with thick rubber mats and two giant rugs woven from heavy mooring lines. We stoop under *Otso*'s bustle. You tread lightly near her, uncertain of how far she has cracked the ice beneath the snow.

'The crew make these mats; you cannot buy them,' Sampo says. A half-woven rug of massive rope plaited over steel cables is suspended above the deck. At the stern the whole assembly, rubber and hemp, is torn, buckled, hackled with icicles and dusted with snow. 'That's where that ship hit us,' Sampo says. 'There's a crack under there.' At the waterline *Otso* wears a belt of stainless steel, which reduces the friction of the ice. The inner hull has been reinforced and reinforced again with tonnes of struts and girders, Sampo says. Thus belted, and with her shallow, rounded keel, *Otso* is descended from the first icebreakers, built on the White Sea in the twelfth century by the Pomor people, Karelians and Russians from Novgorod. They navigated in *koches*, flush-planked sailing vessels with rounded keels. They were designed to be squeezed. Pressure on either side of the hull would pop them up on to the ice, undamaged.

Tem and Sampo fly the drone, gathering publicity footage. Its cameras relay shots of us standing in a wave pattern of snow like tide lines on the ice, which is blown clear here and there, shining black. I think all three of us are missing our children. You want children out here, to run and point, to shout and marvel, to skitter on the ice and laugh at the drone, to chase and flee from it. We would caution them about looking anywhere near the sun. A glance in its direction is met by a shattering silver glare, the snow throwing the light outward and skyward: the albedo effect. To experience the albedo is to stand in a still storm of light and radiation.

On a day like this around 90 per cent of solar radiation reflects off the snow. If the snow ridges or hummocks, the albedo drops to 80 per cent; when the temperature climbs above zero the snow dulls, pools appear and 50 per cent of the radiation is absorbed. When the ice melts open water reflects only 10 per cent of the radiation and the planet warms. It is estimated that the loss of summer sea ice and its albedo in the last forty years has raised global temperatures as much as if humans had emitted 25 per cent more carbon dioxide in that time.

Fast feedback, as this process is called, creates warm air over water where before there was cold air over ice, so snowlines along Arctic coasts retreat, leaving bare tundra. While the radiation effect of the loss of albedo over ice is known (having been measured by satellite) the equivalent calculations for the tundra have yet to be made. Satellite imagery reveals that in high summer there are now six million fewer square kilometres of snow than there were in 1980, with a corresponding loss of albedo. At a certain point the loss of snow and ice albedo will drive global warming by so-called radiation forcing. This direct heating by the sun of a planet whose reflective polar shield has melted means the effect of any additions or reductions in atmospheric carbon dioxide will make comparatively little difference. We will enter the stage of runaway warming. Loss of albedo is the biggest threat to our existence, according to this model. We have not reached runaway warming yet; we stand on diminishing ice, thinking of our children, in the era of not yet, barely daring to guess at how soon. A sober date for soon was given by the British Met Office in June 2016: 'Models vary in their ability to capture recent changes in the Arctic sea ice, but climate projections from models that perform well against observations of past climate show that a plausible earliest date that the Arctic could be seasonally "ice-free" in a given year is the 2040s.'

High in the blue above the drone, satellites are preparing to capture images of the maximum extent of the year's winter ice, which occurs in early March. By the end of the month the results will be published and reported: ice coverage will be the lowest in the thirty-eight-year satellite record. 'Truly uncharted territory,' the UN World Meteorological Organisation will say. 'In thirty-five years I have never seen anything close to what we've experienced these past two winters,' the director of the US National Snow and Ice Data Center will comment. Scientists and newspapers will conclude that the influence of human activities on the climate system has become more and more evident – as if it had not been evident for forty years, as if there were still a reasonable doubt, as if by repeating the obvious with more and more evidence, deniers and the indifferent will be brought to a place of sudden realisation, after which humanity will work as one to make planet-saving alterations to our behaviour.

As seafarers know, disaster unfolds this way. The concentration with which Sampo, Arvo and Ville perform even small course changes is a function of the habitual vigilance of sailors familiar with the rhythm of misadventure: slow, slow, quick, very quick. The mass and momentum of ships mean that by the time you begin to make urgent changes the point at which they could make any difference has passed. I have seen it on small craft and large – the apprehension, the small alteration, full comprehension and the sudden reversing of engines, the spinning of the wheel, the crunch.

With the Paris Agreement of 2015 – setting a limit of two degrees temperature rise above pre-industrial levels, while recognising that 1.5 degrees is what is actually needed – humanity signalled its apprehension and a willingness to make adjustments. Paris envisages a 'ratcheting up' of ambitions to reduce climate change. Beneath this approach to our custody of the planet is the tacit understanding that as a race we require disaster before we make dramatic change. The rallying cries of the environmentally and socially minded echo around the Internet, but we all know the calculation much of the world is making, though you never hear it said: better our great-grandchildren run out of planet than our children should lack for whatever we can grab for ourselves and them.

Toting the drone and its control boxes, we straggle back to the ship like children returning from kite flying, the temperature sinking with the sun.

CHAPTER 7

The Coast of Lapland

W<small>E MAKE</small> for the northern corner of the bay, where the port cities of Tornio and Kemi are the transit points for cargoes travelling to and from Lapland, north-east Sweden and Murmansk on the Barents Sea.

'The ice has thickened,' Ville announces with a restrained urgency which I think signals delight. 'There's no open water in the north.'

Tem is on the phone to his fleet. Ships are sticking and queuing, icebreakers stuttering, a vessel is trapped in the middle of nowhere and Sampo is buoyant.

'Kemi-Tornio is a kind of chaos. A vortex, and we are here on the event horizon ... but being drawn in!'

'*Polaris* has lost one of her engines,' Tem says, 'so we will go and cut this ship free, and *Polaris* can come down and do Raahe.'

Polaris is in her first season of operations, the most powerful Finnish icebreaker afloat and the first to be partly powered by liquid natural gas.

'Where's this lost ship?' I ask.

'She's out here ...'

On the computer her icon is a little box with a dot and a vector line out in the middle of a black screen.

'Hurrah! Action!'

Pushing north at full power seems to charge the bridge with a euphoric vandalism. Smashing ice, dazzling half the night with our searchlights and listening to Radio Nova is joyous. Nova is relentlessly sunny, playing Bon Jovi and Belinda Carlisle, music from the time of the first alarms over the Antarctic, the thinning of the ozone layer. Through simple legislation – the banning of CFCs – the hole healed. It can be done! Change can come! And if not, stuff the emissions and God bless the ice! A ship is stuck – what else matters? *Polaris*, the cleanest, greenest most advanced icebreaker in the world, has a teething problem. Great! Bad news is good news, the worse the better.

'What happens when you get storms?' I ask Sampo. (I love a storm.)

'At twenty-five metres per second we close the gulf at the Åland Islands. That's it. The VTS and the coordinating captain shut it down.'

The VTS, the vessel traffic service, manages the passage of ships in the gulf. Wind at twenty-five metres per second is forty-eight knots, fifty-five miles per hour – a force ten storm on the Beaufort scale.

'Then everything stops. In 2011 you could wait thirteen days, iced in. One ship we pulled out, they'd been there so long that their agent in the port said, "We're going to call the police on you." "Ha ha! You're very welcome!" We moved ships in convoys of eight that year. The Russians do it differently. They get thirty ships together with a couple of icebreakers and move them all. But then when they get to port they have to wait again for everyone to go in and out.'

Ville explains what will happen when we reach the trapped ship, a small chemical tanker on a run between Sweden and Finland.

'So we pass close to her, go around her, and then she can follow our track. If we are moving quickly the ice around her breaks.'

'How close?'

'You have seen the stick?'

The stick is a plank a couple of metres long poking out of *Otso*'s starboard side. It is marked with red and black stripes ten centimetres thick, allowing the helmsman to peer down from the bridge, compare the stripes to the profile of broken ice shards and estimate the thickness of the pack.

'We went so close to one the stick broke, but we didn't touch.'

'Crumbs!'

Ville has a way of signalling amusement without smiling.

'Look …' He brings up a page of photographs on a screen. Here is a steel strut which you might just bracelet with two hands, cut in half by a breaking towline. Here are bulbous bows crunched by impact. Here are bent and twisted gunwales.

'When the tow breaks …' I wince.

'You don't want to be near. We take risks every time.'

It is said with matter-of-factness, not pride. The pride is in the doing of the thing.

'You can spend your life at sea and never steer the ship,' Sampo says, 'Autopilot all the way to port, and then the pilot comes on board. But we are almost always on manual. If you go from icebreaking to a merchant vessel and anything happens, you don't hesitate. You switch off the autopilot and steer.'

There is a crystalline brilliance in the moonless darkness. It is a night for shooting stars, for planets suspended like portents, for strange lights and for those who

> ... follow the Night-Hag when, call'd
> In secret, riding through the Air she comes,
> Lur'd with the smell of infant blood, to dance
> With Lapland witches, while the labouring Moon
> Eclipses at their charms.

In *Paradise Lost* John Milton deploys the night-hag and the Lapland witches as an earthly measure for the followers of his Satan. By the late seventeenth century, when Milton was writing, the 'witches', Saami shamans, were having their sacred drums burned and their ritual trances proscribed by Christian missionaries inspired to zeal by this last redoubt of European paganism. Witch trials were held and rewards offered for the surrender of the drums, which led to a boom in their manufacture. Fantasies of child sacrifice and orgiastic gatherings so terrible they eclipsed the moon reveal more about imaginative Christian excitement at the wild possibilities of paganism than they do about innocent reindeer herders: the Saami were believed to be able to summon the wind, to direct curses by spitting on a knife and touching the victim with the spittle, to possess second sight and mysterious powers of connection with the forest and sea. Something of these powers attached themselves to all Finns, according to sixteenth-century accounts, which have sailors being offered winds for sale, tied up in knotted ropes.

The sea tonight lies black-glazed, white reefs of snow-dust lying in waves across the ice. Arvo is at the helm, a grandfatherly man who meets your gaze over his spectacles. His regard is stately and amused. Arvo is a Swedish-speaking Finn; as a young man he worked on boats between the mainland and the Åland Islands.

'Then I was going there for training and I met my wife. And then it was container ships. I would be away for six months; it's OK when you are younger.'

'And then?'

'Ah, my wife is from the Åland Islands. There have always been many sailors there. She is quite fine. I did many trips between Europe and South America. I was working for Chiquita; it was a good company but they

went into bankruptcy in 2001. One ship I left, my friend
rings me up – "Arvo you've got to come back! We hit a
rock!" I said in the middle of the Mediterranean you hit
a rock? You can't! But they did. Huge torn hole in the
bow.'

'So you prefer icebreaking?'

'Now we will see!'

The trapped ship is *Ursula E*, a small orange tanker
lit up like a prize in a trophy cabinet, no longer than
we are and much lower in the water. Arvo does not
reduce speed at all as he angles in towards her stern.
She has been running her engines, keeping her propeller
turning; there is a clear patch of turbulent water behind
her but she is dug in hard at the bow. Closer, closer we
go. Ville comes over and stands behind Arvo, whose
concentration is palpable. For all his years at sea, Arvo
is still catching up with Ville at the helm. Ville is feeling
the ship through his feet, chewing gum and gazing as
if he is concentrating for Arvo, willing the older man
to make the perfect pass. The shock of our passage
splinters the ice fifteen metres perpendicular to our
stern. Arvo performs a tight skidding turn, towing
destruction around the tanker; we look down on her as
if swooping in by helicopter. The cracks fly out across

the ice, linking the ships, shattering the sheet and setting the tanker free.

'Full ahead and follow my track,' Ville tells the tanker over the radio.

She takes up station behind us.

'How was that, Arvo?'

With a laugh he looks over the top of his spectacles. 'Fun! No one else can play with big ships like this. Only icebreakers can do it.'

Between ten and midnight, high in the gulf, we have crossed Sampo's event horizon and reached a kind of icebreaking bazaar. We lead our tanker past a stuck ship, *Transvolante*, whose icebreaker has turned away to help someone else. *Transvolante* will follow us. Coming down from the north is something like a fallen star, a white explosion of light which turns out to be *Polaris*. She looks almost frightening, her array of searchlights are swords of light. Now there are more lights, and two more ships, the icebreaker *Sisu* and her charge, a trim blue German tanker. We sidestep the blue tanker, our orange *Ursula* following, and the blue tanker heads south in our tracks. Now we turn away, intending to hand *Transvolante* over to *Sisu*, but in the ice between us *Transvolante* sticks. *Sisu* backs around her then cuts in front of her and on they go, but as we back towards our new charge, the blue German tanker, *Transvolante* sticks again. *Polaris* and *Sisu* reverse.

Now three icebreakers appear to be willing one trapped ship to move. We can all push a ship backwards, stern to bow, but cutting them out in reverse does not work so well: manoeuvring astern at low speed is tricky and does not generate enough wash or shock to shatter the trap. The icebreakers talk to one another in Finnish, but there is a lot of Finnish silence too. It is not anyone's place to tell anyone else what to do, exactly. From a distance we must look like a convocation of sea beasts, eyes glaring, in a stand-off over prey. Arvo and Ville say little but their expressions are eloquent. *Come on.*

Before midnight the new watch comes up, Sampo and Villi-Matti, wishing everyone good morning.

'How do you like your visit to Lapland?' Sampo asks.

'It was sweet of you to lay on all these ships!'

Good mornings are exchanged on the radio, as if daytime and daylight are unconnected. There is a professional solidarity in this company of the night, a resolute cheerfulness in the net of voices across the gulf. Fatigue and mockery are kept away from the radio. *Atle*, a Swedish icebreaker, asks us for work. Whoever is on her radio sounds hopeful more than expectant, a bubble of amusement under a slightly forlorn request. We have to say we have nothing for her at the moment.

'Swedes are scared of Finnish ice,' says a watchkeeper in the dark on the port side of the bridge. 'They want Swedish hairdresser ice.' (The Swedes are manifestly scared of nothing, and *Atle* is desperate to be involved.) 'They will be laughing at Finland again. We have one ship being repaired so we have hired them to come over to this side. If there's not enough work they will laugh at the stupid Finns ...'

Two centuries after it ended, the six-hundred-year period of Swedish rule still leaves a chip on some Finnish shoulders, clearly. Finnish jokes require Swedes to be the butt, as Swedish jokes need Norwegians.

Eventually *Transvolante* is freed. She follows us closely through the ice and the small hours as we steam south, *Polaris* trailing us until we pass Oulu, where she turns away, her formidable eyes still blazing, heading for a foxhole, as the icebreakers call their parking spots in the pack.

CHAPTER 8

Care of Ice

MARITIME LANGUAGE has a lovely way of writing place and approximate position on featureless water, making the sea's face legible. We are in Raahe's roads, also known as its roadstead, an indeterminate spot a couple of nautical miles from port where ships can anchor in relative shelter. Behind us, seen from land, is the offing, which is the further part of the sea, the more distant view. It is a pearly day of soft horizontals, silver bars of sky above, black leads streaking the ice. *Otso* grinds through a narrow fairway choked with a mush of ice boulders, *shuga*, Sampo calls it, pronounced *shoo-gar*, using the Russian term for this rubble of ice balls, grease ice (freezing slush) and mashed-pancake ice. The battered Dutch bulk carrier behind us slows to pick up pilots and finds she cannot move. We back up and flush her clear with a blast of wake. She sticks again. This time Sampo reverses to contact with her bows and pushes her backwards. She is running her engines full ahead to keep the propellers clear of ice but *Otso* does not notice. Now she stops a third time, a stew of *shuga* heaped up against her bows.

'See,' Sampo says, patiently backing again. 'Every time we use the fairway we churn the ice into balls like this, and then more balls, and then they are linking up. So at the end of the spring we are actually making ice. The last we have to break will be in the fairways into the ports.'

Tem surveys the trapped Dutchman. Behind her the air is so clear you feel you can see the curvature of the earth.

'In Kemi they save some clean ice where they can go when the channels are filled,' he says.

'You are making and breaking ice at the same time? Isn't this a very weird job, Sampo?'

His age still eludes me; he has a boyish face and a rigour in his dress and presentation that is almost naval.

'When I was a student doing environmental science I was working in this bar. It was a very hot day and I was holding on to these two pumps and I thought, *I really should have something else to hold on to.* So when I was twenty-four I went to sea. It just shows you, a small decision on a hot day can send you to north-east Greenland! And now I have the master mariner's certificate.'

'Are you a natural sailor?'

'Well I'm good at details. My wife says I never remember anything important, just details. But our business relies on details, settings, numbers. I have a second job, renovating at home, but it's not voluntary. It's mandatory, by my wife …'

The Dutchman makes port, and we turn north again as the wind rises under a sky threatening deep cold. Heading between two patches of thicker ice we cross *nilas*, the transparent crystal skin of the new freeze, shining liquorice black. As our wake carves through the *nilas* ripples of our passage swell under the surface, lifting the crystal sheet into flashing zigzags as the flat solid meets the rounding liquid. Crossing the pack we cut through fault lines, ridges of broken and frozen slabs, lucent green dusted with snow. By the time we make Oulu roads the conditions are extraordinary, a slit of pale light to the south, a dark bar across the northern sky, and between them a rainbow vault of cloud shading from blue through greys to black.

A cement carrier is jammed in *shuga* which has filled the fairway. As we lumber up to her, stern to her bow, there is no water visible; she looks like a toy left lying in a white sandpit.

'We will tow her,' Tem says. 'It can take time if they are not very used to it, but we have had this one before. Maybe twenty minutes to get the lines on.'

Down on the main deck the bows of the cement carrier overhang us, her lines and chains hackled with icicles as though the ice is climbing her. Three figures in luminous jackets move slowly on her forepeak; below, two of our crew toddle ponderously in the bulk of their jackets, cold and caution making them seem hesitant and robotic. The windchill is minus nineteen, numbing your face in four minutes. The gap between my leggings and socks is a frigid slash. The cold makes you move slowly, think slowly. In the lee of a stanchion I shiver, watching a dance in which only two out of five figures can move at a time. Our crew throw up heaving lines, which are attached to monkey's fists, heavy knots like cricket balls, the most complicated in a sailor's repertoire. Above on the cement carrier the heaving lines are drawn in, taking heavier lines and then steel hawsers with them. The hawsers are attached in a Y-shape, with the tail our main towline, a reassuringly brutal cable of corded steel. It takes a slow while before they are satisfied, then all crew withdraw, ours stringing a chain across the deck behind us beyond which none may pass. We return to the shelter of the bridge and watch as Ville puts the tension on – one pull, two pulls, testing.

'She's not right there,' Ville says, and the starboard side of the harness is askew. 'She'll hold.' He inches the power on, the lines straighten, a shiver of locking tension running through them, and, first by inches, then by feet, we move.

At five minutes to midnight the snow comes, blowing from the south-east, port to starboard across our search-light beams in a pouring silver current. Above the beams the snow is invisible; below the bridge windows it is a flying carpet. Reidun is a good photographer, but even her camera cannot catch the whorl and witchery of the blizzard. The comfort of the bridge is an extreme counterpoint: dressed for Sunday breakfast, it seems, we eat cake, make tea and survey screens. Our range of vision stretches to twenty miles on the AIS, the automatic identification system, but we have another machine aboard, the J-Map, of which Sampo is particularly proud.

'A real-time system linking Finnish and Swedish coastal radar,' Sampo says, zooming out until we can see the Gulf of Bothnia and the Gulf of Finland, the coasts and main seaways hedged with a forest of tiny boxes, each with a vector line indicating vessels and their courses. 'It's a naval system. We don't have access to their information obviously – we can just see course and speed – but you can see men of war on it; you can't on the AIS because they have their transponders switched off. But when we move out of the range of Finnish coastal radar the navy can see what we can see.'

'So we become a listening post?'

'More like watching, another radar ...'

Feeling that we are not quite like other ships is an obvious source of pride. The icebreakers are owned by Arctia, a corporation belonging to the Finnish state, and the sense of being a strategic asset matters. The J-Map is not linked to other systems on the ship in the hope that it will not be hacked. The Finnish position of 'active neutrality' during the Cold War was layered with ironies which extend to the present. It was clear that in the event of war Finland would be a battlefield: the Russians would come over the border, and the Americans would attack them with tactical nuclear weapons. The obliteration of Finland was incidental.

Norwegian and Swedish soldiers and American spies made tours of Lapland, identifying junctions, bridges and radar stations which would make nuclear targets, according to the Finnish former soldier and intelligence specialist Jukka Rislakki. He tells the story of an American attaché at the Helsinki embassy whose 1962 tour of Lapland, measuring roads, bridges and borders, was so brazen that his hosts asked him to leave. A decade later the American naval attaché announced that he planned a similar tour of the harbours of Raahe, Oulu and Kokkola. Finnish security service officers were astounded by the sight of a spy openly photographing their harbours from a boat but took no action. Washington and Moscow both made it clear to Helsinki that they were not interested in the south of the country, only in the shortest routes across it – to the Bay of Bothnia in the middle, and to Norway via northern Lapland, Sweden being neutral. This cannot have been much comfort to the Finns. Their response was practical.

'Every building bigger than thirty thousand cubic metres has to have a bomb shelter,' Sampo mentions as we discuss the Finnish position.

'Still today?'

'Oh yes. Mostly they are the parking garages. You can store bikes and things there, but you have to be ready to have them cleared in seventy-two hours.'

'Where's your nearest?'

'My daughter's school. It's two hundred metres up the hill.'

I knew it. They *are* future-proofed.

We watch the tracks and courses of freighters, Sampo clicking in and out, half the Finnish coast under his fingertips one second, the next a small knoll under shallow water on our landward side.

'Ah, this is *Sisu*'s knoll,' he says. 'They were following their own track back this way, but the ice had moved north, so they went over it. The depth there is eight metres!' *Sisu* draws 7.7 metres.

The movement of huge sheets of ice defeats perception and intuition. Fast ice forms a rime around the bay, locked in place by attachment to the sea bottom or the shore; seaward the pack becomes a broken tortoise-shell of shifting plates. In March 1809 an entire Russian army left Vaasa, a hundred miles south of us at the bay's narrowest point, crossed the ice and attacked Umea in Sweden. Travel on ice roads around the bay and out into

the southern gulf was common, and an arresting experience for visitors. In February 1779 William Coxe, historian, priest and traveller, set out into the Gulf of Bothnia.
He spent the night on an island: 'In the evening a violent
hurricane came on; we heard on all sides the cracking
of the ice sounding like explosions of thunder.' In
sunlight the next morning, the storm having produced
'several apertures' and the ice melting, Coxe made for
the Åland Islands on a perilous thirty-five-mile sleigh
ride. His guide 'carried a hatchet and plumbing iron'.
Coxe describes this unnamed man cutting ice and measuring thickness, making 'considerable circuits' and
constantly shouting and warning the sleigh drivers. 'He
often called out to the drivers to keep at some distance
from each other; and repeatedly warned them to follow
the precise track which he pursued. In this manner he
conducted us without the least accident, to the Isle of
Aland.' Coxe's tone is in marvellous contrast with the
presumed feelings of that guide, who appears to have
duelled physics for eight hours with such skill that his
charges felt only serenity.

CHAPTER 9

Frankfurters, Death Traps, Droids

IN A blizzard of small flakes we run through ice, cracks jumping a hundred metres ahead of us as we head for the middle of nowhere, as Ville puts it, to retrieve a seventeen-thousand-tonne Swedish tanker carrying chemicals to Oulu. The noise at the bow is thunderous, and the ice is various today. Its mottled archipelagos are made of black curving runes, blown clear, and ridges of glowing green slabs. Behind us sea smoke forms in our wake as the water is exposed to the frigid air. We lead a second tanker to the oil terminal at Oulu, the wind whistling and weeping around the bridge. Sampo was on tankers.

'Those guys die at fifty from a multitude of cancers,' he says, shaking his head at the ship behind us. 'That chemical stuff, it's on everything – your clothes, your skin, your boots. You can change and wash and maybe you still bring it into your home. At least they are stable – good ships in the North Atlantic. We had seas breaking over the whole deck. All you could see was the foremast. The only ones to really stay away from are the ore carriers, two to three hundred metres long. Because of the shear forces they break and go down in a few seconds.'

He tells the story of the *Finn-Baltic* pusher and barge. On Christmas Day 1990 she left Raahe heading south with a cargo of iron ore which according to the dock workers was already wet and shifting. The captain nursed her south on one engine, keeping her speed low to prevent spray breaking over the forecastle and further soaking the ore. As the weather worsened they needed more power and manoeuvrability. The second engine engaged, more water came aboard and the ore began to liquefy. Around twelve thirty on Boxing Day afternoon, rolling in heavy seas, *Finn-Baltic* took on a two-degree list. As she was turned into the wind the sludge of ore shifted in a mass.

'She capsized,' Sampo says. 'Everyone but two guys died. The engineer had stored a torch and a bottle of

Coca-Cola in the propeller shaft tunnel. When it went over they climbed up there. They banged, and the rescuers heard them and started cutting the plate. Pressure blew the plate fifty feet into the air and the two guys got out.'

Only later, researching the accident, do I make the connection. *Finn*, the pusher part of the combination, and the barge, *Baltic*, were raised, rebuilt and sent back to sea, renamed *Steel* and *Botnia*. I know *Steel*. We all know her – the sinister black ship with her brute bows and winged bridge like a submarine's which has been taking coal into Raahe. You do not introduce a ship by her accidents, but the fact that *Steel* has capsized and lost all but two of her crew – I am certain it was in Ville's mind as he introduced 'the ugliest ship in the Bay of Bothnia'.

Reports of the disaster are grim reading: the bodies of drowned men retrieved from the office, from the staircase, the shower; the remains of the pilot and captain found in the drift path of the wreckage; the deckhand's body never recovered. The details and inferences are almost worse. The crew spending Christmas at sea in vile weather, leaving Raahe with a wet cargo, driven by the pressure to deliver. The cautious push down the coast, the captain discussing with the pilot whether or not to wait for better weather. The wind slackening, inviting them on, then strengthening again. The captain staring always out of the bridge screens, dreading every wave which dumps seawater into the hold, and making his turn for safety too late. The chief engineer told the investigation that he had long planned to head for the propeller shaft casing in the event of a capsize because he knew that with the cargo gone the single-hulled vessel would float. Clearly he also considered the ship vulnerable to capsizing. It is easy to forget, unless you work on them, that two ships sink every week.

I look at my shipmates with new eyes. Ville, son of the chief engineer who went all over the world and who tried to take his boy whenever he could, bringing Ville aboard at three years old. When he has the controls his gaze is never still; he sweeps the horizon, the instruments, the screens constantly. ('I've spent much time in the UK,' he comments. 'Hull, Grimsby, Immingham. I only saw the sun twice.') Sampo reels off the years and certificates it takes to become a master mariner: 'So by the time you get to an icebreaker you have done five years on the kinds of ships we work with. You know what it is like to follow. To steer a big ship you have to feel it in your arse – if you can't feel her movement in your arse you will never be good at manoeuvring! You feel it long before any instrument will tell you.'

Tem recalls some of his time on cargo vessels. 'Raahe is the toughest place. The worst weather. And *shuga*! I had two days stuck in Kemi roads on a shit ship with no food. The crew were the strangest people. They were all total misfits.'

'People go crazy,' Sampo says. 'One Finnish captain invented his own words. Leads he called something like ri-leads for some reason. He used it stubbornly all winter on the radio until it started to catch on! People talking about ri-leads ...'

Tem identifies with this. 'I had to do a daily weather bulletin in English, so I used to look up the most archaic words I could find. I knew I had won when they had to ask me what I was talking about.'

We cackle. All Tem's stories conclude with a self-deprecating coda.

'But I am very silly. Off Greenland I got pneumonia from swimming in the Arctic,' he confides. 'I had a temperature of thirty-nine degrees. I couldn't leave my cabin.'

'We didn't notice,' Sampo says. He produces a picture of the crew swimming in the Arctic as a man stands on the ship with a rifle, on the lookout for polar bears.

'Working up there – blue ice everywhere and a big ship behind – it's a death trap.'

At lunch we face the national dish, if you believe Tem, which I am unsure I do, a pile of split frankfurters filled with cheese. Queasy, I have another go at the fruit bowl, a pyramid of desiccated satsumas. Lasse offers a tour of his engine room. Lasse is the watchkeeping engineer. He has a gentleness and a sadness about him traced in webs of wrinkles. I see a gnomish quality in his grin, but that idea may just have been planted by the deck officers.

'You know it's spring when you start to see the gnomes on deck,' they say, referring to the engineers.

'They call the engine room Nut Valley,' says Lasse, issuing fat ear defenders. He leads down stairs, through heavy doors, towards the noise and heat. The engine room is a series of low steel compartments confining a battering roar, a frenzied shaking force which seems desperate to escape the tangle of machinery. To communicate we lift one of our earpieces and yell, or signal like divers.

'We carry fifty thousand spare parts,' Lasse shouts, opening a store in which crates of bolts shine like treasure. There are silvers and coppers, steels and brasses, angular turnings, rounded stalks, objects pressed, plated and cast. Behind another door the noise is suddenly a yammering assault.

'What do you actually do down here?' I scream near Lasse's ear.

'The motorman patrols, looking for leaks, checking, monitoring. We work twelve on, twelve off.'

'Are you busy?'

'Sometimes! We have fuel leaks, water leaks.'

There are racks of tools from a steampunk fantasy, a xylophone of copper hammers and giant wrenches stolen from trolls. As we squeeze along the green steel walkways Lasse gestures and shouts as if he is introducing members of a venerable and subterranean crew who are not allowed out any more.

'Four generators – six thousand volts. Rudder hydraulics ... Main engine cooling ... Fuel purification – we use low-sulphur marine diesel ... Desalination ... Converters ... Heat exchanger ...'

Here are pop-eyed gauges, domed centrifuges like droids, vines of copper piping and sprouting thermometers; the fuel pumps are entire oil refineries in miniature, budded with bolts and flowering stop-cocks. A serpentine hissing comes from the fuel uptakes as *Otso* drinks her endless fill. At the sewage filtration system Lasse pauses by an encrusted window in a settling tank, peers in at what looks like the liquefied and sulphurous innards of a cadaver. He produces a jug and draws off a familiar-looking fluid which he sniffs.

'This is urine,' he says, satisfied, and dashes it into the bilges. He invites me to inspect workshops and edge across a gantry above the twin propeller shafts. The main bulkhead doors are hydraulic, hand-pumped open and shut, a reminder that we are below the waterline, and any ingress of the Baltic here would take us to the bottom. As we move forward the engine noise dips, overlaid now with the grinding cacophony of the ice. As we circle back, the engine tattoos the beat of its pistons into my chest, my feet and my inner ear.

'Yes, it is a very dangerous place to work,' Lasse says. 'We have very good medical care, the best you can buy.'

'The best you can buy' also defines Finland's approach to public health, where standards of care lead the world. The key is the country's system of all-inclusive health centres, dreamed up by radical doctors in the 1960s and launched in 1972. The health centres provide the entire population with all the basics: 'all-inclusive' covers dentistry to ambulances, from GP-run hospital services, rehabilitation, environmental health and home nursing to student healthcare. Some centres are now merged with specialist hospitals and integrated with social welfare services. In 2002 a law was passed insisting that all patients, urgent or not, should be assessed within three working days.

At first Lasse made me think of a doleful clown from an antique time, but now I think he is a more like a monk, the guest master of the monastery, the one whose duties permit and compel him to talk to strangers, to the world of people unfit and unformed to understand the fundamentals, let alone take the vows. To me the wonder of the engine room is barely removed from the mysteries of faith. Ville touches a button eight decks above us, and a thousand things react, the shining axles spin and the propellers turn.

'On one ship heavy fuel oil exploded in my face. It was a hundred and twenty degrees. I had second-degree burns. Without the medical care I wouldn't be here. I am sixty next year!'

We withdraw to the engineers' control room, a large cabin on the main deck which everyone passes on their way to eat. The watch spend a great deal of their time in front of the screens in here, eyeing systems schematics, monitoring points and following the rest of the world through social media. There is a particularly large television hanging over us, showing the Nordic World Ski Championship, which has been casting a growing spell over the crew and the ship. Finland is hosting, and *Otso* is supporting the national effort, silent crew assembling to watch whenever they are off duty. Cross-country skiers power through a pine forest above his head as Lasse reclines in his chair.

'Yes, I have been frightened many times. The mind goes narrow. It's obsessive. You want to follow your instincts but that's very dangerous. Instincts are not for the engine room. It's very stressing, quite the same as firefighters have. But they train and they have protection. You have to think very quickly what to do. The frightening thing is when you are icebreaking and you have a big ship behind – you have all the engines on full and something goes. Because she can run over you. I had a fire off Alaska, a grey-water pump was burning.

I decided quickly. I called the bridge, I said don't let the alarm go off in the cabins, we have it under control.'

At the memory Lasse swells his cheeks and exhales a slow puff, mimicking the way he must have forced himself to calm down and think. If he makes a mistake he could cost the crew vital minutes; being right keeps them from the dreaded continuous bell, the ship's fire alarm, which brings everyone to the muster station in whatever clothes they can grab, imagining the worst – the particularly hellish worst is fire in an icy sea. Fire is the reason you study the cleanliness of a ship when you first board.

'We had to shut the doors and find a route out through the air conditioning for the smoke. Electrical fires are very poisonous.'

'How do you cope with the fear?'

'You know *The Lion King*?'

'Yes?'

'Shit happens and you just try to survive.'

Disney must have injected some of the country's bluntness into the film when they dubbed it into Finnish.

'There was one ship, a tanker, she was junk. But the engine room was very clean. We were taking oil between Wilhelmshaven, Shetland and Liverpool. We had many swells, it was very rough. It was leaking all the time in the engine room but the crew were very good. One ship I hated, I hurt my back, burned my face.' He scowls. 'And the chief engineer was Finnish, he was very nasty. He never washed. He was an arsehole. We were taking oil from Algeria to Fiumicino. There were two Russians, number two was all right but number one was very strange. Every morning he took me by the sleeve and led me somewhere.' He assumes a high, lilting Russian accent. '"Lasse please, clean this!" And then the sleeve again. "Lasse please, clean this!" He wasn't a bad person but I hated it. That was just *hateful*.'

In his vehemence he has coiled forward in his chair and you can feel that ship's magnification of his irritation and resentments, the steel bulkheads bouncing his annoyances back at him, the roil of indignation inside him as he was plucked by the sleeve, the escalation of the ship's torments a misery. I change the subject, asking about Algiers. He saw little of it.

'Do you have a favourite port?'

'Trieste!' he says immediately, and his hands go up behind his head. 'Trieste was wonderful. I was so relaxed when I was there. I love their Italian humour. And you know cabs in Trieste are very cheap from the port, and they are honest,' he says, searching my eyes as if for confirmation. Taxis matter to seafarers. The first money you spend after the weeks or months spent making it ought not to be stolen or squandered.

Lasse laughs suddenly.

'The Filipinos say the best view of a ship is in the back window of your taxi as you are driving away.'

CHAPTER 10

Long Friday

Friday is just over an hour old and the bridge is an intertwining of dim screens, darknesses and subdued bulbs. The beams of our searchlights illuminate glittering curtains of snow. I love coming up the last stair into the shadows and atmospheres of the bridge, to the night's strange theatre and the feeling of half-forgotten, half-stolen time. The world never seems so asleep and so elsewhere as it does on the bridge of a ship during the late watch.

'Good morning!'

'Good morning! What are we up to?'

Sampo has cut a barge out of ice in the fairway and turned south.

'A ship and pilot are waiting to come out of Fish River, the pilot wants an icebreaker and the north end is confusion.' He points to a symbol with a cursor.

'*Atle* has been trying to free her and she's stopped. *Sisu* is— What's *Sisu* doing? Chaos! The pilot wants to know when we'll get there. You know rule number one of icebreaking?'

'Go on, tell me.'

'Never give them a fixed time. Everything will change and the time never works out. There was an attempt by a tech company to coordinate it all through an AI. It failed completely. The wind direction, the different kinds of ice, the speed of the craft, sticking or not – incalculable variables.'

A Finnish cover of 'Yellow Submarine' plays on Nova. Sampo claims the words have been changed to 'Let's all break ice.'

Sampo changes places with Villi-Matti. The chief is the only officer whose shyness I do not quite dare assail. A tall, lean man with close-cropped hair, he concentrates on our heading with particular attention when I appear. When we steam through darkness or mist the navigating officers enter a kind of trance, the body engaged on maintaining course and speed, the mind in that half place engendered by long-distance driving. The helm schedules are relentless. Arvo and Ville are on from 6 p.m. until midnight and 6 a.m. until noon, with Sampo and Villi-Matti taking the other halves of the clock. I dread being the tic, the tug on the sleeve, that dims Villi-Matti's voyage. There is something drawn about him which asks to be left alone. I do not blame him. A non-seafarer with a notebook, clogging up the bridge, asking questions ... His pairing with the loquacious Sampo is a neat balance.

Tonight Sampo discuss Finland's defences and military posture, the recent purchase of howitzers from South Korea and the proposed acquisition of fighter jets from the US. The Finnish government is cancelling land purchases by foreigners near Finnish airports and bases, he says.

It turns out a number of these transactions were registered to Russian companies with no business interests in Finland. The sense of shadow-boxing is palpable: is this comic paranoia or outlandish war game? Is there a difference now? From the bridge of *Otso* it feels absurd and bizarre even to contemplate conflict in the region. The entire idea seems to belong to a suddenly chaotic land-based life. In comparison the sea is so simple, its demands

so clear. In the gulf tonight are Russian sailors relying
on Finnish icebreakers; the coast is lined with Finnish
ports loading Russian cargo. The strength of nature here,
the sea's rude laws and the rule of the ice make curios-
ities of nationalism and flags. No wonder Russian
oligarchs are so keen on very big yachts. The sea remains
the last place to which you can run away.

By the time the light returns there is a skewering bitter-
ness in the air. The wind has veered, pushing the ice
southwards. We go with it, setting course for Kokkola,
which was once a famous front line.

In 1854 Kokkola, known then by its Swedish name of
Gamla Karleby and locally as the Town of a Thousand
Sails, was a major port selling tar and timber to the great
maritime powers. The absurd Crimean War brought
British warships to the Bay of Bothnia to blockade the
gulf and deny these strategic materials to the Russian
empire.

It was a peculiar campaign. In Raahe (then called
Brahestad) ships, timber, warehouses and tar were
torched. In Kemi landing parties burned two miles of
stacked timber. The word went down the coast that the
British promised to burn naval stores but not private

property. Many Bothnian traders did business with the British, spoke English and considered the raids harsh treatment. With Finnish stoicism they parleyed with the attackers, offered no resistance and watched the destruction. The British kept their word, sparing a Cossack barracks in Oulu, then called Uleaborg, for fear the fire would spread to Finnish buildings. A huge pyre was made of shipbuilding materials the British said belonged to the Russian government, but the townsfolk still felt sufficiently well disposed to the raiders to send fresh provisions out to their ships. According to the naval historian Andrew Lambert, some of the material destroyed in the attacks was the property of British merchants who, four years later, were still trying to obtain compensation.

In Kokkola the presence of Russian troops and the very shallow approach to the harbour brought out the locals' *sisu*. The warships could not get close, negating the threat of bombardment, and British demands backed with threats to destroy the town were rejected by a delegation led by a merchant, Anders Donner, who owned stores and warehouses the British were proposing to burn. In small boats the invaders advanced into an ambush. Seventeen died and thirty-nine were wounded or taken prisoner. The rowing boat which now occupies the English Boathouse in Kokkola's English Park was stranded and forced to surrender.

It was a 'melancholy catastrophe', according to the British vice admiral in charge of the Baltic fleet, who was blamed for it. To the Russians it was a triumph, propaganda proof of the fraternity between Finns and the tsar. Anders Donner was invited to the coronation of Alexander II. To the Finns it seems to have been an extraordinary moment. A local hero was made of Matts Kankkonen, a seal hunter who killed a British officer with the first shot of the ambush. His portrait by Wladimir Swertschkoff still hangs in the palace of the president of Finland. Matts does not look comfortable in the picture, standing rigidly, one musket in his large right hand, a second weapon thrust awkwardly through his belt. A medal hangs from his hunting coat like a target. With a British warship stranded on the horizon behind him, Matts seems somewhat weighed down by resolve, his blond fringe as severe as a monk's and his bony face set. As painted by Swertschkoff, Matts is part of that chain of inadvertent warriors which stretches through the civil war, the Winter War, the Continuation War and onwards. By his distant gaze you might almost think he knows it.

Kokkola took its victory with exemplary seriousness. Prisoners were invited to balls, the wounded were cared for, and the graves of the deceased are tended to this day, their maintenance paid for by Britain. The meticulous local museum records that there was one injury on the defending side, 'a horse which had to be put down due to a broken leg'. The British seem to have taken the defeat with typical idiosyncrasy, issuing a series of requests for the return of the captured boat. Kokkola turned them down. The marauders returned the following year, fired enough ammunition to make their point and withdrew.

There is something in the Bothnian campaign emblematic of the absurd and thudding destruction which great powers visit upon the world, no village too small, no port too distant, no local trading relationship too minor to be blown or burned away. While historians such as Lambert might be right in praising the Bothnian blockades and raids as strategic successes (Sevastopol was taken in the same month the British returned to Kokkola; the deployment of Russian troops around the gulf may have contributed to its fall, Lambert argues), the disasters in the Crimea erased the entire Baltic campaign from the British national memory, its events overwhelmed by the tides of butchery on the Black Sea.

There is a telling detail in the story for an icebreaker on the way to Kokkola this Friday afternoon. As they made their way along the same track we are using, the heavy British paddle steamers struggled through ice thick enough to smash boards out of their paddle wheels. It was 29 May. Such thick ice endures so late in the season only in the far north now.

We begin our approach to Kokkola through mist, trundling into an opacity of ice and sky. Sea smoke in our track is the overture to Bothnian fogs.

'In springtime for days on end you can't see *squat*,' Sampo says, evidently delighted with the word. 'Sometimes it's so low down, the bridge is above it while the rest of the ship is covered.'

We make the port in blowing snow, Sampo spinning us on our axis, breaking open the mouth of the channel. Vessel movements and the discharge of cooling water keep the inner port clear.

'I like this tradition,' Sampo says. 'Look at the bow.'

Otso performs a skidding pirouette, shuddering slightly, leaving a rubble of ice chunks nodding in a slew of black water. The port is a line of chimneys, a steel mill, a zinc-smelting plant and a small dinosaur herd of cranes loading a carrier from pyramids of iron ore. *Otso* comes to rest. Postprandial stillness descends; we are digesting pork and potatoes in cheese. Peace permeates the corridors, the air conditioning mumbling softly.

In their control room the engineers are watching ski jumping. On other channels are *Emmerdale Farm* in Finnish, a loopy sketch show involving a man dressed as a kind of owl-priest with wing mirrors, and *The Voice of Finland*, an *X Factor* spin-off. The ski jumping is the pick of it. We watch the Ladies Normal Hill Individual competition, hypnotised by the long floating fall of the jumpers, their landings, apparently identical each time, and the gentle repetition. To an expert each second of launch and flight must be a fascinating compression of craft, athleticism and skill, but to us the only variations are the colours of the competitors' suits and their reactions. Ski-jump spectatorship seems to turn on whether a helmeted head shakes in disappointment or a gloved fist punches the air. Watching it is like being in a tribute to Sartre's *Huis Clos*, set in purgatory rather than hell, where placidly we study people experiencing strong feelings.

I am getting better at diagnosing silences: this is an almost interested, almost contented silence. As long as the ski jumping lasts we are licensed to sit in a relatively easy companionship of introversion, nourished by the tiny variations of engagement which filter through the screen to us, the minute distillations of the emotion of the jumpers. When a Finnish competitor appears there is a ripple in our shared atmosphere, I think. She launches herself, swoops down, rises off the ramp a hundred metres up, sets in the air and flies. The crowd cheer, hoot and warble. Eighty-six metres and four seconds later Julia Kykkaenen returns to earth, slows, turns and acknowledges her supporters with a wave. She finishes in nineteenth position, a good effort in a sport which turns out to be dominated by Germany and Japan.

'Well done, Finland!' I offer.

'Ey ...' someone responds.

('What is the difference between a Finnish extrovert and a Finnish introvert?' runs a local joke. 'The extrovert stares at *your* shoes when you talk to him.')

It is an afternoon for reading *The Year of the Hare* by Arto Paasilinna, published in 1975, an enduring classic in Finland, a hit in France, filmed twice and translated around the world. Vatanen is a journalist on an assignment with a photographer, 'two dissatisfied, cynical men, getting on for middle age' in Herbert

Lomas's translation. 'The hopes of their youths had not been realised, far from it. They were husbands, deceived and deceiving; stomach ulcers were on their way for both of them; and many other worries filled their days.' On a dusty midsummer evening they run over and injure a hare. Vatanen sets off after it, shedding wife, job, possessions and all constraints in an odyssey through the succour and cruelty of strangers, forest fires, military manoeuvres, pagan rites, a love affair and various encounters with vets. The imperturbable Vatanen, always accompanied by his hare, discovers passion, rage and obsession, embarking on a homage to Moby-Dick in pursuit of a murderous bear which leads him across the Russian border, a one-man dismissal of the Cold War. (The Russians turn out to be delightful: 'On behalf Red Army, congratulations! Now I arrest you as spy. But no worry – this formality. Have drink.') The reader emerges from the book gently sluiced of the irritations of the age. To be 'profound in reflection' is to do right by the situation before you, regardless of social norms; to be 'benevolent in disposition' is to balance your rights with those of others (including hares), unshackled by received thinking. To be both is to be a true subversive.

Paasilinna's critique of a Finland comically in hock to regulation, time-serving, convention, authority and acquisition is the same as Sartre's in *Huis Clos*: *L'enfer, c'est les autres*. Sartre's three immoral sinners in a comfortable hell learn that their punishment is to crave redemption from each other; reliant on the esteem of others for their self-worth, having mistreated others and now having no choice but to see themselves and each other unalloyed – there is no blinking in this hell – they are trapped in an infernal eternity. Similarly, Paasilinna explores the idea that hell is not the existence of other people; rather it is self-subjection to their opinions. Vatanen walks out of his grinding job, bad marriage and all convention in a moment of existential inspiration: the injured hare matters as much, as little, as anything; caring for it punctures the absurdity of normative ideas about what a life is and should be. Ceasing to care what his wife, employer or anyone else thinks of him sets Vatanen free. With the hare he finds an apparently ludicrous but entirely pure relationship where self-worth is not dependent on another's judgement. Perhaps Finnish taciturnity is a reaction to the torment of self-definition through the opinions of others: if I say nothing you have less by which to judge me, and I have less from which to suffer.

Finland is deeply involved in the question of how self-made hells can be alleviated. Depression and suicide rates are high by European standards, as they are in Norway and Sweden, where well-being and general happiness are also high. The happiest nations have the highest suicide rates. Researchers speculate that this may be a consequence of perceptions of relative inequality: being surrounded by the apparently happy makes the unhappy feel worse. In Europe suicide rates rise as you travel north-east and fall as you reach the Mediterranean. No doubt it is a coincidence that temperature, quality of food and loquacity all rise as the rate falls. No doubt it is also coincidence that European suicide rates and Internet use – the most powerful device for exposing the individual to the apparent happiness and the judge-ment of others that it is possible to conceive – are both highest in the Nordic countries, and lowest in Italy, Spain and Greece.

By half past eight the ice is a pristine field, and the mist has fallen back to an orange luminescence behind the chimneys of the port. A tangerine glow is cast queerly through the driving snow by the small blazes of the harbour lights. I do not find isolation frightening when experienced alone, but isolation shared, being cut off together, seeing your own solitude reflected in another, feeling another's loneliness like a pang in you, like a dread third force – these are shivering things. The chimneys smoke but there is no sign of human agency, as if the towers and lights were erected long ago then left. There must be a canteen, a control room; there must be men working the smelters. There is something heroic in the gaunt scene: how many little industrial outposts on how many anonymous shores are keeping their lights burning tonight?

A Dutch cargo carrier, *Flevoborg*, has been loading all day. She comes out now, low in the ice, steam, snow and orange light billowing behind her. The pilot boat sets off into the white, looking like a snowmobile moving over the pack. Behind *Flevoborg* is a much bigger ship, red and black, loading iron ore. She looks like something from another time, as if she has sailed out of an archive, austere and haunted.

'The wind is coming from the north-east,' Ville murmurs. 'Ideal for ice formation.' He has taken over from Arvo, keeping us just offshore, not easy in the wind and snow. Ville seems to feel the want of work, the want of ice most keenly. There is something about Ville, in his standard grey tracksuit and sandals, the way his bulk moves swiftly, the way the others defer to him despite his shyness. I understand it now: sea time and something else, some deep relationship with his role the others do not quite have. There can be five master mariners on this bridge: Sampo and the silent Villi-Matti work together; Arvo, a grandfatherly man, is paired with Ville, and Tem comes and goes. But when Ville handles the ship I have caught the others watching.

Quietly, when we are away from them, Tem says, 'Ville is amazing. I love watching him teaching Arvo. He doesn't *say* anything.'

We take *Flevoborg* out to the edge of the ice. Open the bridge wing door out here and you stand in a truly frightening night, the snow riding horizontal on a fierce wind, the sea moving strangely in all directions, as if stirred and swirling. Pancake ice knocks against the hull and there is loneliness and peril everywhere.

Now we wait and wait. I turn in late and we are still standing by. Sailors have always waited, like truckers and train drivers, like anyone who has worked on the conveyor belts of trade. In a half-dream before sleep I am wheeling

through a future of outraged nature, of deserts of heat
and cold in which machines work and humans monitor,
where the environment is vengefully dominant, forcing
us to live like Finnish seafarers – behind glass, monitoring, waiting.

CHAPTER 11

Bright Weekend

DAZZLING SUN! The sky is purest white-blue at the horizon, rising by degrees to a glowing lapis blue overhead. All the ship's smells are sharp in the morning air: whiffs of diesel, sulphur and cooking, and the blunt smell of steel. Seaward, the ice field runs to the end of vision, only the channel buoys breaking the white, frozen in their lurching. In all the pristine immensity only a raven moves, carbon black, flying out to an island of pines like a ragged priest bent on establishing a mission. A fisherman appears in a yellow hovercraft, steering towards us then veering away as if he can detect Ville's move towards the megaphone. 'We don't accept visitors,' Ville says with a comical growl. We talk about books; the ship has an excellent library of thrillers and classics in Finnish, locked in a cupboard and not much read.

'I have made a book,' Tem reveals, 'part of a book. It is called *Ninety-Nine Shades of Grey*. That is what it is. Ninety-nine different greys. They crowd-funded it. The third shade in the book is called Maja after my wife.'

I look at Tem with delight and some disbelief.

'The Finnish sense of humour in a book! Was she pleased?'

'Oh yes, she likes this very much. It has an ISBN number and it is in the Library of Congress.'

'What kind of grey is Maja?'

'Very pale. Like ice!'

There is no work, it seems, so a straggle of engineers and deck crew head for the gangway. At the bottom of the ladder it takes only a couple of kicks to break through the skin of snow to a slush layer on top of the ice.

'We think this is safe?'

'Yes, yes, we will measure it!'

We proceed, toting an ice drill, a measuring stick and the drone. The ice is twenty centimetres thick, we discover, and they make me repeat the measurement in

Finnish: *kaksikymmentä senttimetriä paksu,* like a riddle or a motto in jumbled verse.

Being out on the white plain brings a feeling of joyful lightness, as though distance and time have lost their grip on being. We wander about, the snow crumping in our boot treads. Sampo flies the drone around and over his beloved ship while I operate the camera. It is kite-flying with a robot, disguised as public relations. We need the cover, in case someone from the world should cross the ice and ask, 'What are you doing? Why are all these men not working?' Ville's grab for the megaphone when the hovercraft approached was revealing. It is somehow part of our identity to be quarantined; we are not ourselves but *Otso* – independent, mighty, mid-voyage and always operational, especially when mooching about in the white.

After an hour someone declares, 'Now it is time we go for one small coffee!' and we troop back aboard. Finns drink more coffee, per head of the population, than any other nation. 'But we like it weak,' Tem confides. 'The Swedes always say they cannot taste it.' I discover the cabin steward, Tom, on a rare break. He is a shy man even by the standards of shy men. 'I worked on supply ships for oil platforms,' he says, 'off Italy, in the Gulf of Mexico and the North Sea. It is not that scary,' he says quietly, 'except the helicopter transfers. You have to do your training in Amsterdam. They put you in a helicopter simulator, drop you in a pool and turn you over.'

As the sun loses its grip on the heights, the snow begins to glow in spectrums of blue. Leads in our wake take on the pale azure of the sky; low dunes of snow are white kraken backs. The smell of ice becomes less indistinct – it is there always, like a premonition of snow – but now it is sharp in the nose when you inhale, a pellucid starkness, an absence, clean and clear. Falling towards the forest, the sun leaves the light citrine. I scramble to the bridge and watch the twilight draw out the colours. In our shadow the broken ice is green as the sky and the ice play the light between them; now the sky is aquamarine, almost green, and the ice green-blues in answer. The sun's retracting flare makes black spires of the pines. You can see the temperature dropping: it is minus five as the sun touches the trees, down from plus one at noon. The sunset still lingers after supper, dim carmines and greens glowing all along a horizon which is minutely serrated with countless trees.

There is a holiday mood on the bridge. The light and ice have shriven us of the claustrophobia of routine. Ville fires up the engines. 'Look, Horatio. Black smoke! That's engine number three!'

A horrible pall of exhaust goes swirling away into the evening. It is funny in a ghastly way, of a piece with Ville's mordant humour. We back out of our foxhole as a small bulker comes out of Kokkola to follow us.

Tem wrinkles his nose at Ville. 'Where do you find all these small ships? You can hardly see it.'

The night fills with stars as we steer west; a satellite crosses fast to the north-east. I am hoping for the aurora borealis, but Reidun summons a site on her phone – the great green nets are far to the north-west of us. Our night is a back and forth of escorting. Kokkola's approaches are marked by substantial structures, concrete and steel beacons.

'Kokkola is notorious,' Tem explains, 'because the fairway is very narrow and there are many beacons. So you should never have a ship unattended. If she sticks and the ice is moving she can be swept into the beacons.'

Sunday's sky is a soft sea of silvers and greys. We are holed up outside Kokkola again. I am looking for someone, anyone, who is doing something interesting.

'We are doing nothing!' says Robbe the deck cadet. 'Drinking coffee upstairs.'

'Everyone onto the ice!' Ville commands, and out we go into an immense and windless silence, a drilling party to establish that the ice here is twenty-five centimetres thick, a drone party obviously, and a shovelling party which Ville leads. They sweep a great H out of the snow and take turns landing the drone on it.

'I was going to write "Tem",' Ville says, 'but too much effort.'

The captain as hero. They are so affectionate and informal with him, and their meticulous attention to their work functions as a protective bubble around him – if anything goes wrong Tem will take the final blame. Although so many metaphors of leadership on land borrow from the sea, the actual relationship of *Otso*'s officers to their captain seems reversed. In his manner Tem retreats from the position of overseer, assessor, wielder of power; instead he sets the larger parameters of the mission, disposing his icebreaking fleet, and the officers fulfil it.

'Every year I do this job because no one else wants it,' he says, coming off the phone to one icebreaker and preparing to call another. 'Things can go wrong, but if they do we fix it! So it doesn't matter.'

Perhaps this is Tem's secret, a fatalistic optimism.

The temperature drops, the cold clamping my head and legs as small squeezed flakes of snow blow through silver light. The cook is smoking a cigar, gazing at the calendars in the smoking room.

'It's nice to wake up and have a cigar and look at these nice women,' he says, his tone paternal. 'I have been on ships since 1976. During the Biafran War I was off the coast of Nigeria. We had people from both sides of the war on the crew. This was terrible, angry all the time. But I am never frightened. I have trust in the captain and the mates; I have trust in what they will do. If you do not have trust it is better you stay ashore.'

'What do you do when you leave the ship?'

'I am taking care of my mother in Raahe – she is eighty-seven. Then in summer we do maintenance in Helsinki and I am still cooking – in the ship; I do not want to cook on land!'

He cannot explain why land repels him, but the money, the habitual rhythm and the contained, simplified nature of sea life must be part of its attraction. In the cupboard of coffee mugs on the bridge is a deeper reason, I think. The mugs are all labelled with the officers' names. *Otso* is not one family, but a network of family groups. The cooks, Penntti and Ulla, and Tom the steward take their meals together. The engineers form a group, the cadets another. Reidun and I, as guests, are assigned to Tem, Sampo, Arvo and Ville.

Two of the cadets have little English, but the third, Katri, is voluble. She is serving as an apprentice repairman, she says proudly, a work placement organised by her technical college.

'I don't want to work on land! Everybody works five days on, two days off, waiting for summer vacation. This is my fourth time at sea. The first was on a bulk carrier, we were taking coal from Russia to Sweden. The sailors were fine! I grew up in a mannish environment anyway. I get along with everyone. I only have two friends really. They keep in touch. Mum was asking, what about kids? What about getting married? I don't have plans for kids so it's not a problem for me. My first goal is to be an officer. This is my first engineering apprenticeship. I find it interesting. I might slide a bit to the dark side.'

'The engine room?'

'Yes!

'So what did you actually do today?'

'We were trying to fix the heat exchanger. And I was working on my own project. I go to dog shows at home so I was making a lead from plumbing beads and flag cord.'

'In the engine room, you were doing this?'

'I don't mind the noise, but if you hear something weird you are on your toes! I finish at four, go to the gym, watch Netflix.'

She becomes suddenly vehement. 'I like ships because I like my *own time*! When you're off duty you can sleep how much you want, watch Netflix when you want. At home I have no time. It started because I had no idea what to do. I didn't want to consider studying at uni, and everything else – nursing, plumbing, car mechanics – no. But then there was a ship simulator and it felt right. The first time at sea was a little scary, but I made friends. I didn't mind all the men. I liked the attention! Boyfriends think it is weird, but that is why you should only date seafarers – ha ha! I have a friend who is a first mate; he does four to eight in the morning so I message him then. The first time I went from Finland to Germany to Southampton on a car carrier. But there was one guy, he told another of the crew I was with him, and that guy started acting weird. I could have started a lot of drama but I promised the first guy I wouldn't say anything because they had four months together ...'

'Did your college prepare you for that side of ships – dealing with the people?'

'They said when you join a ship the first impression really matters so you have to be really open, tell everyone who you are. The first time I was most worried if I would be seasick.'

'Is it all as professional as it seems, Katri? No parties, just work and Netflix? I thought I smelled vodka ...'

She laughs. 'Not on *Otso*, but my friend was on a ship, they were at sea for five weeks and she was only sober for two. They were on the Atlantic side of Norway and she was really ill. But this wasn't seasick, this was hangover!'

'So you don't miss all that?'

'We will dock on Thursday. I will probably be drinking then. On Friday I am going dancing – foxtrot, cha-cha, tango. I like long drinks. Do you know long drinks? Gin and grapefruit ...'

* * *

Katri's ease and confidence in this male world is in line with the great tradition of Finnish women's self-realisation. They achieved universal suffrage in 1906, the first women in the world to be able both to vote and to run for office. Their standing in society was noted by Ethel Brilliana Tweedie, who travelled around the country in 1897. Her story of the trip, *Through Finland in Carts*, is suffused with humour and insight and a joy which is extraordinary, given her circumstances. Her beloved husband, Alec Tweedie, her father and her dearest friend all died within the space of five months in 1896. She and her two children were bereft and ruined, her husband having lost his fortune before he died, and her father dying intestate. But Ethel Tweedie was emphatically unbroken, although her journey was made in deep grief. This is as much of it as is allowed into the pages.

Grave trouble had fallen at my door. Life had been a happy bounteous chain; the links had snapped suddenly and unexpectedly, and solace and substance could only be found in work. 'Tis often harder to live than to die. Immediate and constant work lay before me. The cuckoo's note trilled forth in

England, that sad, sad note that seemed to haunt me and speed me on life's way. No sooner had I landed in *Suomi* than the cuckoos came to greet me. The same sad tone had followed me across the ocean to remind me hourly of all the trouble I had gone through. The cuckoo would not let me rest or forget; he sang a song of sympathy and encouragement. It was on a brilliant sunny morning early in June that the trim little ship *Urania* steamed between the many islands round the coast to enter, after four and a half days' passage from Hull, the port of Helsingfors. How many thousands of posts, growing apparently out of the sea, are to be met with round the shores of Finland!

And with that she is off, curious, delighted and very funny. In Helsinki she observes Finnish women working on building sites. Later in her account of the journey she presents her conclusions.

In fact, one cannot travel through Finland without being struck by the position of women on every side. As no country is more democratic than Finland, where there is no court and little aristocracy, the daughters of senators and generals take up all kinds of work. Whatever the cause, it is amazing to find the vast number of employments open to women, and the excellent way in which they fill these posts. There is no law to prevent women working at anything they choose.

Among the unmarried women it is more the exception than the rule to find them idle, and instead of work being looked upon as degrading, it is admired on all sides, especially teaching, which is considered one of the finest positions for a man or woman in Finland. And it is scientific teaching, for they learn how to impart knowledge to others, instead of doing it in a dilatory and dilettante manner, as so often happens elsewhere.

We were impressed by the force and the marvellous energy and splendid independence of the women of *Suomi*, who became independent workers long before their sisters in Britain. All this is particularly interesting with the struggle going on now around us, for to our mind it is remarkable that so remote a country, one so little known and so unappreciated, should have thus suddenly burst forth and hold the most advanced ideas for both men and women. That endless sex question is never discussed. There is no sex question in Finland, men and women are practically equals, and on that basis society is formed.

Eight years after Mrs Tweedie observed women labouring on a building site in Helsinki, working-class women were organising and participating in the 1905 general strike. Nineteen were elected to parliament in the country's first elections, nearly a tenth of all MPs, with the first female minister taking office in 1926. In 1991 Finnish women broke the world record for representation in a national parliament, occupying seventy-seven out of two hundred seats. In 2000 the country's first female president was elected (Tarja Halonen served two terms); the first female prime minister, Anneli Jaatteenmaki, came to power in 2003. By 2007 over 41 per cent of elected MPs were women – a figure achieved without quotas. Quotas do apply to the boards of municipal authorities, governing bodies consisting of elected officials and companies majority-owned by the state, and equitably so: the Finnish definition of equality is 40 per cent representation of each sex. Since 1991 more Finnish women have voted in elections than have men. Though there is more to do – women have only marginal influence over Finland's economic decisions, for example – the progress of Finnish women towards equality is a story of rapid advance.

Farming in the Finnish wilds of the early nineteenth century allowed for little distinction between the agency and influence of men and women. Twentieth-century wars and a fall in the male population required the advance of women into the workplace, with many staying in paid employment. Finnish innovations in childcare have been crucial to the success of this story: in 1973 legislation funding and obliging municipal authorities to provide day care created a new professional class of family childminders, allowing parents to return to work after generous leave. This was followed by a home care allowance, paid to parents looking after children under school age. Parents can now choose between home care and day care. Two-thirds opt for day care and return to work.

Mrs Tweedie made observations about Finnish men too. Though overtaken by time, genetics and political correctness, they remain a pleasure to read.

The Finns, though intellectually most interesting, are not as a rule attractive in person. Generally small of stature, thickset, with high cheek-bones, and eyes inherited from their Tartar–Mongolian ancestors, they cannot be considered good-looking; while the peculiar manner in which the blonde male peasants cut their hair is not becoming to their sunburned skins, which are generally a brilliant red, especially about the neck where it appears below the light, fluffy, downy locks. Fat men are not uncommon; and their fatness is too frequently of a kind to make one shudder, for it resembles dropsy, and is, as a rule, the outcome of liqueur drinking, a very pernicious habit, in which many Finlanders indulge to excess.

In 1919 a large section of Finland's women voters used their ballots to support a prohibition on alcohol which lasted until 1932. One can only sympathise with the prohibitionists. In the long winters it must have been galling indeed to watch a proportion of your household income disappearing into your husband's liver, inflaming his face and temper. Ironically the percentage of house-holds experiencing this misery was low – Finns consumed an average of half a litre of pure alcohol annually, which made them a relatively dry nation. The problem was that the popularity of home distilling and a culture among those who did drink of hitting it heavily meant a very high rate of alcoholism. A hint of how booze gripped the nation is given by prohibition's exemption of drinks containing less than 2 per cent alcohol: they were not considered strong enough to count.

Many Finns, Mannerheim among them, were opposed to the law, and many broke it. Mannerheim was law-abiding of course, but he could afford to go abroad, and did so whenever he could during the 1920s. Cafes selling special tea – vodka served from teapots into teacups – became immediately popular. Home brewing ballooned, leading to a hundred thousand annual arrests. National per capita consumption doubled to a litre a year. In 1930 a million illegal litres were seized; at the end of the following year 70 per cent of voters chose a return to the legal bottle.

The culture which brought about prohibition is still alive, according to the World Health Organisation, which reckons up to half of Finnish men participate in 'heavy episodic drinking'. Katri's 'long drinks' are a curious relic of the end of prohibition. In 1952, anticipating a tide of thirsty foreign visitors for the Olympics, the landlords of Helsinki hit on the idea of mixing flavoured soda with hard liquor, and the long drink was born.

Downstairs in the mess cupboards is an archive of how seriously the comfort of *Otso*'s officers and crew was taken when she was equipped in 1986. There are ranks of wine glasses, brandy flagons, shot glasses and glasses for aquavit, all polished, housed in special shelves and never to be used again. The only legal bottle we have aboard is the broken neck and cork of the champagne magnum which was smashed over *Otso*'s bow on the occasion of her launch, displayed in a special case. The curation of memory is important and touching. The lounge, with its comfortable chairs, red upholstery, card tables and soft lighting would be at home on a cruise ship, but is never used now. Ghost stewards serve aquavit to ghost officers, but the room is kept lit and ready, as clean as it was left when the last drink was taken, before the surrender to laptops and tablets and downtime spent alone in cabins.

By Sunday afternoon we are working again, escorting out of Kokkola, escorting back in to Kokkola. *Bloody Kokkola*, I think, *will we never be set free?* The ice is moving, squeezing, thickening. At one point the mouth of the fairway wears thick red lipstick where it has chapped the paint off one of our charges. Through staves of blowing snow low clouds magnify the sun, diffusing its rays in penumbras of bronze and silver.

Lasse takes me down to the engine room to watch a work party tackling a broken heat exchanger. Katri is there with another apprentice, both observing studiously as planks of wood are strapped across the grilled sides of the wardrobe-sized steel box in an attempt to stop it leaking. It seems a valiant effort, as though the engineers are splinting the exchanger in a spirit of hope, reminiscent of my own DIY.

'It is increasing our oil consumption,' Lasse shouts. 'But we have fifteen thousand litres aboard. We will be OK.'

'What does it actually do?'

'Cools the oil!' he shouts. 'If it blows up there's hot oil everywhere.'

'And you fix it with wood?'

'We can get spare parts in two weeks. So we pack it. If it comes apart it will do more damage.'

'Lucky we have the planks.'

'Ah, Finns are very expert with wood! I got my first knife when I was five and started cutting my fingers ...'

* * *

Up on the bridge Tem is thinking about sea-level rise. At present the whole of Finland is lifting, post-glacial rebound raising the level of the country ten millimetres a year, while sea-level rise is about three millimetres globally. This difference is being eroded as glaciers melt and warmer water expands, but the closer you are to glaciers the less you are affected because under the thinning ice, relieved of its weight, the earth's crust is rising too. In Finland, not far from the Greenland ice sheet, this will mitigate the consequences. Tem's complaint is that the global average is of no use to mariners or coastal dwellers; wind, tide and air pressure render all but local measurements irrelevant.

'I think sea level should be absolute,' he declares. 'It is impossible to calculate! It is never the same anywhere. But if it was absolute then we can say the land goes up and down.'

'The land here is going up, isn't it?'

'Yes,' Reidun confirms. 'It is most extreme in Bothnia – one centimetre a year.'

The Finnish Meteorological Institute predicts a ninety-centimetre sea-level rise in the Gulf of Finland by the end of the century, but a mere thirty centimetres up here in the Bay of Bothnia.

'Is Bothnia interesting to a geophysicist?'

Reidun gives one of her long looks. 'It is dominated by older basement rocks, which is interesting for mining on land but not for exploration.'

There are Paleoproterozoic rocks, she says, nearly two thousand million years old, and small-scale tectonics like dolerites and ores.

Her sense of utility is tremendous. She deals in aeons of time like a player shuffling cards; all 'exploration' is undertaken in the name of oil; rocks are interesting for what they can yield and the physical challenge they offer. Reidun is a climber. There is a trimness and compactness about her fleeces, jeans and trainers: you can see her on an expedition, first to strike her tent, ready to lead. When she shows Sampo or Ville new tricks in the database operating system she has the manner of a teacher whose attention elevates the pupils' confidence, gently prompting so they seem to make the discoveries themselves.

'I love the world!' she says. She takes a photograph of the ice and the notched line of Kokkola's chimneys hemming it to the sky.

At seven thirty the *Eeva VG*, a trim blue cargo carrier, leaves her berth and takes up station behind us. It is minus twelve outside. In the peeling cold constellations glitter. The fires of Orion, the Plough and Cassiopeia are so bright they blue and hollow the darkness between them, as though you can see the depths and deeps of space. Between the ships black water smokes silver.

Half an hour later Ville is on the phone to Tem.

'Problem!' he says, and emits a burst of Finnish.

Roars of laughter come from the phone.

'She has been going full speed ahead and now she has a cooling problem,' Ville says, 'so she is broken down in the middle of the fairway, and there's another ship coming out.'

'Can we tow her?'

'No no, not allowed. We can only tow for icebreaking! Not for breakdowns.'

'She needs a tug?'

'She needs a tug. Or a good engineer.'

We stand by. From Ville's disposition it is clear that there is a point when the law of the sea, to give assistance to those in distress, will trump Finnish regulations applying to icebreakers and tugs. After a while *Eeva* begins to move again. We lead her out to the mouth of the channel and turn aside into the ice.

I am beginning to develop a feel for the ice now, as I circle the deck in the freezing dark, listening to it. It is like weather, like rain or mist, in the way it comes upon us according to its own laws. It is like the sea in its tenacity and its restlessness, in the way it moves ship tracks, grapples down buoys, traps stragglers and climbs hulls. It is like rust, like entropy, in the way it sidles aboard, rinds the rails with icicles, patches the decks and stiffens the ropes. But in its reformations and renewals, in its unpredictability and its beauty, ice is all but alive.

'The frost performs its secret ministry,' Coleridge begins 'Frost at Midnight', an image of holy work in some middle place between life and thought, between the perceptible and the immanent. Fascinated by ice, Coleridge would have seen how quick is the creation of ice ferns on a windowpane. The first crystal puts out arms which grow arms of their own, each sprouting off at sixty degrees to the root. The name for the process, dendritic growth, refers to the tree-like appearance of the structure, the living plant perfectly echoed in the ghostly imprint of the crystals. Nature's patterning leaps across that boundary we think of as the absolute.

CHAPTER 12

Frozen Monday

B Y DAYBREAK the temperature is minus ten and falling in defiance of the morning; the frigid air seems to slow the rising of the sun. A long dawn flares in spectrums of red and orange across the horizon; the ice in answer lightens from deep green to pale magenta. The defiant flourish of a lone gull beating towards the shore seems to emphasise the desolation of this place. I have woken with a clutch of worries in my gut, a sailor's condition – fears for your family, worries about children, about education and money and chances and what will happen to them if something happens to you? I scold myself and assume my working face.

'The whole Bay of Bothnia is frozen!' Tem announces, delighted. The captain is transformed, no clowning or

self-mocking now, his voice deep and quiet as he briefs
Arvo and Ville. The first business is lifeboat drill. We
assemble in minus eleven, bulked up and waddling on
the open deck. Ville calls the roll. We answer our names
and don life jackets, their straps tangling gloved fingers.
For a moment we are all fiddling helpfully with someone
else's jacket, a conga of fumbling. Doing this in the dark
with the ship heeling would be chaotic but at least we
can say we have practised it. The faces of the crew are
set against the cold and the routine.

'Move to the sunny side,' Ville orders, and we troop
over to the starboard lifeboat. We gather around a life
raft.

'Attach the line to the ship before you throw it over
the side!' he says. 'You pull this here and tie this on.'

'Not practising getting into the lifeboats, today, Ville?'
I ask.

'More people are killed and injured doing lifeboat practice than are saved by it,' he says. 'If we start going down
get into an immersion suit. That will give you six hours.
Otherwise you lose consciousness in about five minutes.'

We stow the life jackets and disperse. Ville allows
himself a rare cigarette. His plan, he says, is a captaincy.

He is a master mariner; the next level is just a matter of sea time and vacancies.

'Icebreaker is a great job,' he says, 'but it is hard with my wife. Otherwise I am thinking maybe a harbour pilot.'

'Wouldn't that be a bit boring in comparison?'

'Jumping on ships in the ice is not boring! And you are based in one port, so you have regular hours and you can go home at the end of the day.'

'But you get more people on icebreakers,' I say, thinking of the cramped capsules of the pilot boats, tiny from our height.

'Ha! I am not really a people person.'

Some mood of contemplation seems to have come aboard this morning, perhaps owing to the lifeboat drill. In the Bay of Bothnia the distance between ship and shore is wider in the mind than on the map. Our futures are held at bay by the duration of the voyage. Sampo is thinking about ice and its bearing on his career. The freeze has set us free of Kokkola; under bright sun we lead a ship north to Oulu as young ice crinkles along the hull. We plan to exchange charges with *Frej*, which is bringing a ship south.

'It's really thin stuff,' Sampo tells Reidun. 'The first hard winds will shuffle it up. It's a bit too spindly for me.'

'Silverado man worries about climate change?' I put in.

He laughs, then his face stills, his expression taking on a look part hopeful, part doubtful.

'We had a briefing from the Finnish Meteorological Institute. They said by 2050 ...' Reidun and I look at him. 'There won't be a need for such a big fleet,' he says diplomatically. 'There will still be winters and some cold ones, but infrequent. But until 2030 they said it will be much as it is now.'

Something of this does not sit well with the realist in Sampo. He shrugs. 'Ships are going to be required to keep emissions down, which means less engine power, which means crappier ships which will need more help, so that balances it a bit,' he says.

'Have you seen a change in the winters?'

'Oh yes. When I started it was the norm for the Bay of Bothnia to freeze every winter – proper ice. Since 2012 it has almost frozen like that, sometimes, but not enough. We get much warmer winters and a lot more wind. It's really noticeable. With the new weather systems what used to be minus three is now plus one. When we were in Greenland it was really warm.'

'The multi-year ice is unlocked,' Reidun says. 'Older ice was coming out. Big icebergs melting off little ones, like pigs around the tank.'

'Before the end of my career I'll have to start selling kebabs,' Sampo says. 'I'll be the captain of a fleet of kebab trucks in Tampere!'

Reidun laughs. 'You know in Norway now they are growing a lot more vegetables and fruit? The forests and the rocks are moving because the permafrost melts.'

'We're getting new species,' Sampo rejoins. 'Wild boar. And Siberian ticks coming over the border. We get heat-waves! Whole months of thirty degrees.'

At supper I ask Ville about the Winter War.

'Does it matter to you, Ville? What does it mean now?'

'It means a lot to Finland! Tiny Finland! The numbers are crazy. There are still a lot of Russians buried under the country. And it means *sisu* of course. Everyone needs *sisu* now. They're making a film of it – another film. There are so many and they are making a big one now.'

We head for Rahja through proper ice, white and bright as a moon, with Ville hopeful. 'The ships will get stuck tonight,' he says. The radios chatter. 'Good late afternoon,' says a ship to a port. (It is half past nine and pitch black.) *Otso* shudders and shakes, cracks leaping three hundred feet ahead of us. Now news comes that a vessel is stuck out in the bay, and we set course for her, wind driving the snow hard across us from the south-east.

In our searchlights *Ostbense* is marooned in obscurity, as if stranded on the salt bed of an evaporated sea. The Russian captain sounds flustered on the radio. It has taken us a while to get to him, and he is late. The pressure on masters to make port on time is constant. All delays are costly, and captains are answerable to machines which monitor their fuel consumption and running times. *Ostbense* is owned by a German chartering firm and flagged in Antigua and Barbuda, naturally. (Flags of convenience save ship owners a great deal of money, owing to less rigorous inspection and investigation procedures in certain territories: Liberia, Panama, Monrovia and Antigua are favourites.) We charge towards her, our engines delivering fifteen thousand horsepower, our searchlights illuminating the wind turbine strapped in sections across her deck.

Arvo will perform this fly-by, his fingertips light on the dial of the rudder control. We stand well behind him. Arvo's view is perfect, *Ostbense* lying trapped below him, snow blowing across her, her wheelhouse dim. It is a vicious night now, the windchill dragging the temperature you experience outside below minus fifteen.

'*Ostbense*, *Otso*. Full ahead and follow our track when you are free,' Ville says over the radio.

'*Otso*, *Ostbense*. Thank you. I go full ahead.'

In we go, fast, passing no more than twenty metres away, the shock and speed of our passage smashing the ice and setting it rocking between the hulls. Arvo slews us around *Ostbense*'s stern and loops back neatly, coming out in front of her.

Ville picks up the radio again. '*Ostbense*, *Otso*. You can use your searchlight to find our track,' he prompts.

'Yes, I use searchlight,' *Ostbense* returns sheepishly, and a cone of light springs from her bow.

'Come on, Russian!' someone comments.

Ville pops his gum.

We feel mighty; we *are* mighty. In the long relationship between the two nations it is rare that the Finns are the more powerful partner.

Now *Atle*, the Swedish icebreaker, calls up asking for work.

'But Tem is not going to let him because *Kontio* is going to do it, so *Atle* can't come down here. We are not friends any more,' Ville says.

Our poor Russian is struggling. 'His speed is dropping,' Arvo says.

Ville goes for the radio again. '*Ostbense*, *Otso*. Are you going full ahead?'

'*Otso*. Yes. *Nyet*. No, sorry. Yes, we go full ahead.'

The voice sounds strained now, a bit desperate, and there is a burst of harsh laughter on our bridge.

'What's going on there?' I ask.

'The Russians, they can be very good, or they can be ... I don't know what.'

We break the way to Rahja. At deck level the noise of the ice is furious, roaring sometimes, so that you look for a low-flying plane. At midnight we lead *Ostbense* in. Rahja tonight is nine lights, two cranes, a couple of storage tanks and wuthering currents of snow.

The channel is menacingly tight. It curves and narrows into a southerly hook, buoys winking close by us on either side. Ville, Arvo and Villi-Matti, three master mariners, are watching a fourth, the ageless Sampo, who has taken over just in time to do the horrendous bit. Having broken a passage almost to the mouth of the port, he must now reverse us back along the constricting, curving channel. The snow has turned the glare of our searchlights into a dizzying white glow, the light bouncing back at the screens. The wind is angry and strong. Sampo handles the ship with a synthesis of calculation, sensation and instinct that cannot be taught or automated. Forces too various and unpredictable to be accounted flow through the helmsman, his body like the reed in a clarinet, turning the mechanical power of the engines and the organic pressure of the wind into movement like a restrained and stately music.

'Reversing *Otso* is my favourite thing,' Sampo says, his tone mild, his speech uncharacteristically slow as he concentrates. 'She just won't go straight at all,' he murmurs, almost to himself. 'This is the part where we dent the propellers. It's really shallow and there are rocks ...'

Inch by inch, somehow, he keeps her in her track.

'Now we turn around.'

He must spin us through the wind in a channel exactly as wide as the ship is long. Every move demands

a countermove – he counteracts each touch of the
throttles and each twitch of the rudder control before
he feels the effects of the initial intervention. You can
sense the others judging, comparing, willing him to get
it right. At such low speeds steerage is all but lost;
control is maintained by a constant juggling, holding
the forces of turn and counter-turn always in dynamic
opposition, pushing the ship by tiny degrees through
her arc. I find myself absurdly thinking of Byron: 'One
shade the more, one ray the less, had half impair'd the
nameless grace.'

Otso turns in her own length. The AIS, the electronic
chart, shows Sampo keeping her precisely between the
lines of the fairway. At some mysterious point the other
officers sense the job is done, and the bridge clears. No
fuss is made, no praise given. Sampo has done what was
expected, but the moment seems to merit more than
satisfied silence.

'I've never seen ship handling like it! How's the
adrenaline?'

'Pretty good!' he exclaims with a burst of laughter.
'Now we just have to go back once more and flush that
last bit of ice.'

And back we go again, until a blast of wake turbulence clears the final ice bar. 'Tradition,' Sampo says, 'and good manners.'

Now we move seaward and pull into a foxhole. *Ostbense* passes, a pilot aboard, almost home. There is a deep satisfaction in the night's work. One more wind turbine reaches Finland; the Russian captain will report its safe arrival in good order to his charterers as *Otso* records another assist, but there is more to it than this. A decade ago a quarter of Russian imports travelled through Finland; five years ago Russia was Finland's second-biggest export market. European Union sanctions against Russia and its tottering economy have inflicted on Finland years of economic contraction and stagnation as she has sought to replace her Russian partnership by pivoting towards Germany. As a result, what was a mutually beneficial relationship is now ambivalent. The old partnership endures out here. For all that we were bullish, we were grateful for *Ostbense*. We needed her as much as she needed us. The flags the two ships fly and the nationalities of the crews are insignificant compared to the achievement of *Ostbense* making port through the clawings of the ice and the driving snow.

CHAPTER 13

Noises at Night

Late-night gossip on the bridge. Sampo explains GM, the measure of a ship's stability. 'Think of it as the force that whips you back up,' he says. 'Some ships carry wood on the deck so that in a very hard roll the wood will go overboard, lowering the GM, so she doesn't go too far. With a very low GM she rolls slowly but doesn't necessarily roll back up! I have been on a ship that rolled thirty degrees, forty-five degrees. When we took *Otso* to Greenland she was rolling like crazy, but we have this engineering miracle, you know.'

The miracle is the heeling tank, a grey rectangular box like an enclosed swimming pool resting on its side behind the bridge. If *Otso* rolls to starboard air is forced into the starboard side of the tank, pumping water into the port side and righting the ship.

A rolling icebreaker, the *Tarmo*, has a place in Finnish history. Her first appearance in her nation's story is March 1918, at the height of the civil war, when *Tarmo*'s crew smuggle Pehr Svinhufvud aboard in Helsinki. Finland's future first president has been on the run in the city, which is in the grip of the Red Terror. Once at sea the Finnish crew overpowers a small force of Russian marines, the garrison of this strategic asset, while they are at breakfast, and *Tarmo* sails Svinhufvud to safety. She reappears, rolls and all, in February the following year.

The war is over, and Mannerheim, interim regent of the new country, must carry off Finland's first state visit, to Stockholm. The *Tarmo* is the nearest thing Finland possesses to an official vessel and has pedigree; firing on a Soviet icebreaker has made her the first ship of independent Finland to engage an enemy craft. Packing a splendid and newly designed Finnish army uniform – one of only four in existence at that point – Mannerheim embarks. He must embody his nation and manoeuvre around the question of the Åland Islands, which Sweden will not give up. *Tarmo*'s rolling, the freezing weather, the thin material of his new uniform and the stress of the occasion make Mannerheim ill. King Gustav offers him a palace for the duration of his stay, but Mannerheim refuses, returning each night to *Tarmo*, where he sweats out his fever. The visit is a triumph. The Åland Islands question will eventually be resolved in Finland's favour. The Swedish press and King Gustav dub Mannerheim a hero.

Tarmo fought on through the Winter War and the Continuation War, was retired, then, like Mannerheim, unretired. The steamer, built on the Tyne in 1907, last broke ice in the dire winter of 1970. There is astonishing footage of her filmed in the 1920s, at work off Helsinki. The ship roars through ice a metre thick as a crowd in hats and coats dances and dawdles around her onrushing hull. A bicycle and a motorbike shoot across in front of her. Men and boys nip out of the way as the bow axes past them. The grins of the boys and the gaily streaming crowd convey an extraordinary relationship with peril. A touch of judgement, quick feet, a bit of luck, and a thousand-tonne icebreaker becomes a plaything.

The times have changed more than the people, judging by Sampo's laughter when I ask him about his adventures.

'Well I was young and foolish. I was on the *Viking Mariella*. Here she is ...'

On the screen he summons up a picture of a gigantic red and white ship, brave and boxy as the 1980s and still sailing today. Two and a half thousand passengers, six hundred cars and the world-record holder for journeys between Helsinki and Stockholm, the ship is an established character in the relationship between the two capitals.

'She had this problem with the anchor. We were going through heavy seas, and when we slammed down into troughs the anchor was banging against the hull. We thought it might come through the side into the car deck. I went out to see if I could bring it up further, make it more secure. When I was out there, this ... *huge* rush of sea came across the decks. I jumped up and grabbed on to a sill on the gunwale. OK, *that was close!*'

'But you felt you had to do it?'

'I wouldn't now! But you have to try.'

Ferry crews have every reason to fear a banging noise in the bows.

'The *Estonia* ...' I begin.

'Yeah. The *Estonia* was a similar ship; she started as the *Viking Sally*.'

Sampo's face darkens at the mention of her name. Originally a Finnish ship, she became an Estonian vessel and a proud symbol of post-Soviet independence. Disaster struck at five to one in the morning of 28 September 1994. The *Estonia* went down in a Baltic gale between Tallinn and Stockholm. Eight hundred and fifty-two lives were lost, the worst maritime disaster in European peacetime after the *Titanic*. Sampo's expression is clouded, angry.

'The doors failed, and they were going too fast,' he says, his hand miming a throttle pressed down. Now he punches a fist into a palm. 'Bang bang through a heavy sea, and the bow doors couldn't take it.'

His anger is a seafarer's revulsion at malpractice. The accident investigation concluded that the doors were under-designed and that the ship should have slowed when noises were heard at the bow. His vehemence is also a rebuttal of the rumours which have attended the sinking – stories involving military equipment, spies and an explosion near the bow. At the suggestion of the Swedish government, the wreck of the *Estonia* was partly buried in pebbles in an attempt to inter her and lay her dead to rest. The site is monitored by Finland and has been aggressively defended by the Swedish navy. Conspiracy theorists allege the wreck contains stolen Russian hardware which was taken aboard with the collusion of British spies. Russian intelligence, they say, wanted the ship stopped and returned to port. The Swedish military confirmed that the ship had been used to transport military equipment on two voyages that September. This, combined with the *Estonia* Agreement of 1995, a treaty signed by a slew of Baltic nations, Russia and the UK, which prevents nationals of these countries from approaching the wreck, has given the rumours an afterlife in articles and documentaries.

That a seafarer should have no patience with the conspiracy theory is understandable. The story of the *Estonia*'s sinking is nightmarish, even by the standards of the sea. The banging, the lurching, the band playing on, then the list and the stairwells and doorways which became death traps, and the cold culling by drowning or hypothermia of hundreds of the unlucky, of the elderly, of the young. To contemplate that the horror was caused deliberately is bad enough, though we know that some governments do not hesitate to slaughter civilians when it suits them. To imagine the collusion of the signatories of the treaty – Estonia, Finland, Sweden, Latvia,

Denmark, Lithuania, Poland, Russia and the United Kingdom – in a cover-up is to lose faith in humanity. Let the doors have failed, you pray. Relatives of Swedish and Estonian victims continue to call for a transparent investigation of the disaster.

Shivering, I walk the decks. Fragmented ice around us is moving in the darkness. It knocks and clicks with a sound like bowling balls colliding. Slabs pile, drift and slip in splashes and snorts of air.

CHAPTER 14

Kalevala Day

'KALEVALA DAY!' I say to everyone I meet. 'What does it mean to you?'

'School ...'

'Yeah ...'

'Not much ...'

The *Kalevala*, meaning *Land of Heroes* – Finland – is the national epic, a collection of story cycles gathered, shaped and embellished by a physician and scholar, Elias Lönnrot, who first published them in 1835. Lönnrot collected the verses on a series of intrepid journeys across the country, eliciting and writing down tales and songs, paying for them, often, with recitals of others he had gathered. Travelling into Karelia, far north and east towards the White Sea through territory which is now in Russia, Lönnrot found rune singers whose memories held thousands of lines of epic poetry. One singer, Ontrei Malinen, a fisherman who contributed four thousand lines, told Lönnrot that his father, Ivan Malinen, would have kept Lönnrot up for weeks, recording all he knew. Ivan could sing for night after night on fishing trips, Ontrei said, and never repeat a verse. The book's beginnings are all music: twelve thousand unrhymed eight-syllable lines, vivid with the rhetoric, parallelism and variation of folklore. There is no earliest date for the roots of this epic singing; the tradition is thought to be at least two thousand years old.

After six hundred years of Swedish cultural and linguistic hegemony (and at a time when Russia held Finland as an annexed territory), it took time for the work's huge impact to be felt. A Swedish translation brought the *Kalevala* to the ruling class, while Lönnrot first expanded the book, then condensed it for use in schools. But during the 1850s and 60s it drove a wave of national romanticism through a nation asserting her identity against the dominance of Russia. Finland now had a masterpiece in her own tongue, establishing Finnish as a literary language.

The book caused a sensation in Europe. Here was an apparently fully formed Homeric myth cycle culled from the songs and stories of the people of Lapland, Karelia and central Finland, bearing few marks of Christianity upon it, carried by word of mouth out of pagan antiquity.

At the centre of the story is the mysterious Sampo, an object forged by Ilmarinen, the blacksmith-artificer who also makes the sky. (Creation in the *Kalevala* is a playful delight: the world is made of shards of duck egg; a dead man is reanimated with the help of a bee.) The Sampo might be a mill which grinds salt, gold and corn; Lönnrot believed it was an idol. Other theories include a treasure chest, an astrolabe, a Byzantine coin press and a world-creating forge. It is the ultimate object – enriching its owner and inspiring theft, pursuit and war. The Sampo's twin progenitors, the hero Väinämöinen and the smith Ilmarinen, seem to represent magic and science respectively, with the shaman Väinämöinen having the best of their encounters – perhaps a projection of the hope of the bard-singers of the original stories that their magic would not be eclipsed. In the Sampo's synthesis of science and magic is the blend of trepidation, wonder and desire that communities in the wilds of Finland must have felt at the approach of technology and the rise of individualism over family-grouped collective endeavour. In the final battle for the Sampo the device is lost at sea.

Our second mate winces slightly at the mention of the *Kalevala*.

'Sampo? You're in it!'

'Yes, this amazing … machine that makes everything, or whatever it is.'

'What does it mean to you?'

'Doesn't it make the sea, the salt? That's quite useful.'

Asking a Finn what the *Kalevala* means to him or her is too wide a question. One of its translators into English, Keith Bosley, sums up the problem: 'From the English-speaker's point of view, the *Kalevala* is the Finns' Chaucer, Shakespeare, Milton, Pope, and Wordsworth rolled into one; but the genius of its sources could neither read nor write.'

No wonder my shipmates look shifty when I ask them about the epic. Even a literature student could be forgiven for blanching at such a compilation, and these boys flew through maths and physics instead. The book is much more influential than read, but Kalevala Day is also Finnish cultural day, the modern history of the

two being indivisible. The *Kalevala* inspired Jean
Sibelius and the work of Akseli Gallen-Kalella, the
country's most prized painter, both driven like Lönnrot
to establish a national mythos. Sibelius drew on the
Kalevala as an iteration of the spirits of Finland and
the wild, the music of nature made myth, in which the
heroes are semi-supernatural musicians. 'The *Kalevala*
strikes me as extraordinarily modern and to my ears is
pure music, theme and variations,' he wrote to his
fiancée in 1890.

Many of Sibelius's best-known works, tone poems,
choral symphonies and orchestral suites are drawn from
the *Kalevala*; his music established the work in the wider
world. The paintings of Gallen-Kalella are much less
well known outside Finland, partly because of the devo-
tion they inspire within the country, where they are
treasured, collected and studied. Few hang in galleries
abroad. From Lönnrot, Sibelius, Gallen-Kalella and
Eliel Saarinen, who designed Helsinki's railway station,
the national museum and a clutch of town halls and
churches, the cultural identity of an independent
Finland flowed. Even our ship has her forebear in the
Kalevala's runes. The hero Väinämöinen first commands
Otso to calm down, good practice when parleying with

bears, then informs him of his cub-hood, a description built on charming observation.

> Sacred Otso grew and flourished,
> Quickly grew with graceful movements,
> Short of feet, with crooked ankles,
> Wide of mouth and broad of forehead,
> Short his nose, his fur robe velvet;
> But his claws were not well fashioned,
> Neither were his teeth implanted.
> Swore the bear a sacred promise
> That he would not harm the worthy,
> Never do a deed of evil.

Väinämöinen also explains that Mielikki, a wise forest spirit, made Otso's teeth from a fir with silver branches and his claws from its golden cones. She 'taught him how to walk a hero, and freely give his life to others', a laudable aspiration for icebreakers, if rather optimistic for bears.

In a climactic struggle on a boat between the ageing Väinämöinen and Louhi, queen of the Northlands, who fights in the form of an eagle, the Sampo is smashed and lost overboard. Väinämöinen is delighted; no more will heroes and witches battle to possess it. This object of terrible power and desire will salt the sea and nourish Finland instead.

> Vainamoinen, ancient minstrel,
> Saw the fragments of the treasure
> Floating on the billows landward,
> Fragments of the lid in colours,
> Much rejoicing, spake as follows:
> 'Thence will come the sprouting seed-grain,
> The beginning of good fortune,
> The unending of resources,
> From the ploughing and the sowing,
> From the glimmer of the moonlight,
> From the splendour of the sunshine,
> On the fertile plains of Suomi,
> On the meads of Kalevala.'

Our *Otso* continues her mission to guard the worthy from harm. We lead *Ocean Trader* towards the pale strip of peeled blue which separates ice and sky. She is *Otso*'s two-hundredth ship this winter, following us through slabs of white mint cake, icing sugar and hard black glass, across which we drive like a chisel, Ville in shades listening to Eminem. Exchanging *Ocean Trader* for *Arne*, we lead another wind turbine towards port. Ville watches *Arne*'s track and calls her: 'Alter course to starboard; you have heavy ice in front of you.'

The ice is in various moods today: crystal slush on the fringes of hard pack, the fairway into Raahe a thick rubble of *shuga*.

'*Arne*. Full ahead, please, full ahead,' Ville urges. She is already close behind us but he wants her closer. 'The nightmare is if she sticks now. It's so shallow here, five metres beneath the keel; it's *shuga* from top to bottom.'

Raahe looks extraordinary, a low line of miniature wind turbines and smelting works steaming under a magnified sun. *Arne* makes port under a penumbra and a swirl of cloud which shades the light from solar orange to black above the conifers.

As we return to the bay, Sampo hands over the controls. Reidun has a go. There is much laughter and much swerving.

'No! Too hard!' she cries as we snake through the white.

My turn. 'Here you are,' Sampo says, 'Steer course 221.'

I have been longing to have a go. I have driven lifeboats, river cruisers, narrowboats and once, making a radio programme about the Parisian river police, a huge crane barge. *Otso* cannot be so hard, and there are no bridges to avoid.

'That dial is your rate of turn. There's your course. All you need is the rudder control.'

The course climbs, 221 becoming 230, 235. We are swinging to starboard. Bring her back and counteract. The rudder control is a small wheel like an ice-hockey puck; tiny touches of fingers and thumb are all it takes. Now she starts to come back to port, the course falling rapidly through the degrees. *Too much! Counteract. Look ahead.* There is nothing, no mark or distinction, from which to take a bearing; only ice and mist. *Anything! Give me anything! A lump in the snow, a ridge, a horizon point to align the bow with. Forget it. Feel her through your feet then.* But my feet are not telling me anything. There are no waves, there is no sensation of wind or pressure on the hull. And the tiller is backwards, of course.

'Look at your rate of turn. She's skidding. Midships. Rudder midships. There's your rudder indicator. Course?'

'Two eighty. Hopeless! I'll bring her back.'

'Move her by increments, counter each move.'

'Easier said ... The autopilot is laughing.'

'Ah, the autopilot is not much use. The ice can drive the gyros crazy, which makes her start to oscillate. We steer all the time.'

'Look, 221!' I hold her for a little while. 'I don't understand how you do it. There's nothing to see and nothing to feel.'

'Ah, but there is. You have to feel it through your arse.'

'I'll have to eat more, then.'

Tem appears and raises his eyebrows at our track.

I apologise. 'The VTS will think you have been hijacked by drunks. Do you even remember your first time?'

'My first voyage was six months on a large crude carrier, a hundred thousand tonnes,' Tem says. 'Between Shetland and Europe. The smell wasn't oil but this inert gas produced by the engine and pumped on top of the oil so that there is never any oxygen in the tanks. It doesn't smell good. Then a cargo ferry between Teesport in Middlesbrough, Hull and Zeebrugge. On the European side communication was no problem. We were all Finnish; they were all Dutch; we all spoke English. But when you get to the UK they can't understand anything we are saying and they are using all these strange words.'

* * *

A quiet afternoon in the ice of Raahe roads turns into an eerie night. Something between low cloud and ice mist surrounds us; above our dimmed lights the vapour hangs like a cave roof. The atmosphere on the bridge is studious, Ville working on a computer, Arvo at the chart table looking like an architect, neat columns of figures in a ledger and his gaze fixed on a screen. In fact they are both shopping. Ville is looking for a new boiler and browsing quad bikes; Arvo is in the market for a house. He surveys prefabricated chalet-palaces with huge balconies, glass walls and windows giving on to rafts of wooden decking.

'Where are you going to put that?'

'It might not be that one – it's up to my wife. At home! On the Åland Islands. Look, I'll show you.'

He brings up a map, and down we go into the archipelago, until we have a satellite picture of a cluster of roofs on the edge of a long creek, pines around them, a neighbour to the north, a little dock, a boat. The pictures were taken in summer. It looks like a dream of serenity in the long green-gold light.

'It's beautiful! Which one's yours?'

'That one. And that one, and that one, the sauna. The new house is going to go here,' he says, and hovers the cursor. Arvo is most of the way to building a hamlet.

'My children come to stay, and there are many grand-children so it is always busy. We sauna, we go fishing and have barbecues. Spring is fishing and relaxing. We catch pike and perch.'

Arvo's dark eyes are made small by his spectacles, but through the glass they gleam. Pride and pleasure radiate from him. A life at sea, and what a lot to show for it. My grandfather was a sailor, his descendants will say to their children. Your great-grandfather was a sailor – he built these houses. From out here in the realm of silence, of introversion, Arvo has made a converse life on land. You can easily imagine his rolling walk down to the dock, children skittling around the lawn, towels hanging over balconies, life, food and chatter. He talks about meeting his wife on the islands, marrying in his thirties and always going away, one of the seafarers of the Ålands who sustain and are sustained by the mirror community of their wives. If you only have half a life on land then what a rich and providing half-life this is. In Arvo's comfortable bulk is the ease of a man who has earned his fortune. I have seen the lightness of a grandfather's smile in my own father, in my partner's father, and now I see it in his. A seafarer like this strikes a bargain with life. You will risk the seas, and yours will be a special loneliness, measured on calendars. The land, which will so rarely be yours, will be yours to give, and if you live, to enjoy when you are done.

'I had a captain once,' he says. 'He came on board and he called a meeting. On his desk he had put a sign. He said, read it. I read it. He said, read it out. I read it out. The captain is always right. Then he said, that is rule number one, the captain is always right. What is rule number two? I said, I don't know. He said, for rule number two see rule number one. This arsehole. Then when he gets into trouble he asks us what to do. We said we don't know, what is rule number one?'

I make sympathetic noises.

'I had a British captain and a second mate, they liked to drink before lunch. And after lunch. Then before dinner, then after dinner until four in the morning! We did everything. It was better they did not touch the ship. They were fine until they ran out of alcohol.'

Ville fires a burst of Finnish at Arvo. They nod agreement and now they are all bustle.

'We've been watching this ship,' Ville says, indicating an icon on the screen. 'She's been struggling. We're watching to see if we need to help her. She's going to Kemi, but ... look.'

The AIS shows her track. She has been drifting and fighting the ice in comical loops off Kokkola. She is currently making less than a knot and going sideways.

'You've just been sitting here, watching!'

'Yes! Ha ha! No, we have to go. You can see there's a big ship's track here. If she could have got there we hoped she could have followed it.'

Arvo presses pairs of buttons, watching the monitors as the engines fire. A deep beat comes up through the deck, and a distinctive high beeping comes from a box beside him.

'Distress signal,' he says. 'A long way away. I was on a Chiquita boat, out from Bishop Rock to Costa Rica. We were across the Atlantic when the US Coastguard called us. They said there is a ship in distress two days north of you and you are the closest vessel, you have to go. We went north for thirty hours before they cancelled the call. They'd got another ship there. So then we turn back. The emails! Days and days of emails.' He shakes his head and rolls his eyes.

He takes the helm and brings us out of our foxhole, hauling *Otso* round in a heeling turn.

Tem has appeared. He laughs. 'Arvo really knows how to take these turns.'

'Remind people we're on a ship,' Arvo responds.

We cross wide leads and patches of ice until we find our struggler locked in a raft of thick ice. The visibility is terrible. Twenty-knot winds blow mist from the southeast. Approaching head-on, Ville can see only blurred lights until we are very close. Ville pulls us in an ankh-shaped loop around the ship.

'Textbook,' Sampo pronounces. 'Straight from the textbook of icebreaking, which we do not have.'

Minutes later we are guiding the Dutch ship through the floes.

'She's a regular customer,' Sampo says of her. 'She's been with us many years. She's an old ship – carries scrap metal and rolls of steel, and random cargo – wood, sawdust. Paper only comes down in big ships. There was one going to Philadelphia today. It has to be really dry so you need some serious air conditioning. They're buying a lot of high-quality timber in Iran at the moment.'

'She's very small.'

'Yeah. Think about it. There's a captain, a chief engineer, a couple of deckhands. They don't sleep at all in twelve weeks. When you meet them they're like the living dead.'

A study by the International Transport Federation found the majority of seafarers work more than eighty-five hours a week, with a quarter saying they had fallen asleep on watch.

The ship of the living dead follows us through the floes as mist scuds across the ice. Now I think of ice as a being – its movements, its agency, the way it determines, yields, thickens, prevents, makes wonderful. I think of ice as Gaia, as world spirit given form and colour. Sea ice can be infinitely studied, tracked and measured, hymned and wondered at; sea ice can be hacked and broken, but sea ice cannot be made by us and cannot be controlled.

CHAPTER 15

Darkness

ENGINES START at seven, the cabins rattling, the ship shuddering and grinding. I wake thinking of Arvo's photographs of barbecues, fishing, boats and the long low sun. I think of a generation retiring under that westering light. Arvo is back on shift, complaining that he has not slept well, looking forward to trying again this afternoon. It is a lissom morning, the light silver-grey, the sea black, the ice a mosaic of green and white.

'Where are we going, Arvo?'

'The same ship as yesterday. Now she is stuck a little bit north.'

The horizons close and retreat with the mist, flat horizontals, as though we are sailing through a two-dimensional world. It is warmer today, the decks sloppy

with snow-melt. There is a tickle in the air like a portent
of rain. Liquefying snow runs down the screens; beyond
them the boundaries dissolve, patches of snow and mist
becoming one.

'Good morning!'

'Good morning, Tem. You are in an excellent mood!'

'Oh I am, fine, fine! I am going home. I have a good
sleep behind me, and it's good to break ice in the morning,
not at 4 a.m. I have sent pictures of us to the VTS.
Normally they only see us on the screen, but now they
can see us pushing, cutting, pulling.'

'It's a disorienting day, isn't it? We could be upside
down.'

Ville grins. 'I had one ship, I said follow my track.
Silence. Then he comes on the radio – "I only see white.
I only see white!" He was from Costa Rica. He had never
seen solid water before.'

'Sometimes they lose concentration when they are
following you,' Tem says. 'They stop navigating. I had
one, I said I am turning away. They were entering the
fairway by the buoys and he says, "I can see a flashing
light! What do I do?" They had no idea where they were.
Sometimes they try to sneak through, they think if they

follow clear leads they will find a way. But the lead goes nowhere, they hit the ice like a shotgun and stick.'

The morning's messages bring news of *Otso*'s next guest in the form of a scan of her passport.

'She is an admiral's daughter,' Ville says.

'A Canadian admiral. We were getting very excited,' Tem puts in.

'But then we got her passport – born in fifty-seven!'

'We should email back, "Why are you travelling on your mother's passport?"'

Skagenbank appears like a black cut-out on a white set. Tem reads the swinging loop of her track. 'They have been following the track we made last night. They have missed it here, tried to get back and ... no hope.'

Ville sweeps us around her. 'Perfect!' Tem exults. 'Ah it is so nice for me.'

Two seals pop out of gaps in the ice ahead. Life at last! They look like fat ladies in black bathing suits, staring as if collywobbled at the appearance of a ship in the middle of their morning swim.

'I think they are making baby seals,' Tem observes.

Arvo shakes his head: 'They have already made them. In spring we see four hundred, five hundred basking on the ice. And then the pups, and then the sea eagles, and then the blood. It's like a slaughterhouse.'

'The small ones, we try to avoid them,' Tem says, 'because they cannot swim yet. The babies look up at us, these crazy people doing icebreaking.'

We keep up our chatter as we cross a black waveless sea, in and out of its shifting cloud which seems to promise hope one moment, despair the next, in a series of slow variations, the moods of dim mulling afternoons and grey mornings alternating. Then the wind comes up and by mid-morning there are waves. Snow, rain and lines of ragged ice fragments like bubbles stream out of the mist. Now the wind keens and whistles as we cross open water. Ville says we are 'scouting the fairway' but it is the equivalent of pacing up and down.

'Too much too warm,' says Arvo. He grabs the pair of hand-strengtheners which sit on a sill by the binoculars and clicks them rapidly. You can feel impatience aboard with us. This is dead time, stretching every minute. It is almost as though we are veering close to another darkness in this sub-polar sea, some ancient dread, like an apprehension of the world's end.

By AD 98 the Roman historian Cornelius Tacitus had heard tell of this place, or read about it in texts now lost. In *The Germania*, his account of the northern tribes, he wrote, 'Beyond the country of the Swedes there is another sea, sluggish and almost motionless, which is believed to be the boundary and limit of the world, because here the last glow of the setting sun shines on into the following dawn, dimming the brightness of the stars.' Tacitus reported that the rising sun might be heard here, and that 'his attendant deities are seen and his crown of rays. Thus far, and no further, does nature go.' The waters of the Gulf of Bothnia and the penumbras of its sun are exactly as Tacitus described them, though his source must have been here in summer as there is no mention of ice.

Pigrum ac prope immotum – sluggish and almost motionless. Yes, this is that sea. I pound around the deck, keeping moving, keeping the cold and rain on my face. On this shadowed day I feel like a sailor's Jonah, as if an approaching depression is coming for me and reaching out past me to the crew.

The psychological responsibility of a seafarer is clear – you must be strong with yourself and wear your bravest face, because ships magnify and transmit moods and there is no way off them. This is why you make Tem the captain, for his miraculous ability to synthesise and broadcast well-being. My task, then, is a trick of language and a question of resolve. On this ship I can admit fear of depression, in the sense of confessing it to myself, but I absolutely will not admit it in the sense of allowing it to come aboard through me. It must not be shown, shared or given a moment of succour. The trick is to see it not as incipient isolation but as a confirmation of solidarity: everyone feels blues and apprehensions; everyone is vulnerable to a tightening of the spirit, whether caused by thought, memory or passing shade. That is what this shall be. The talking-to I give myself before returning to the bridge is the equivalent of Ville's insistence that we are not prowling up and down though stippled black water, dissatisfied and redundant. As I return he parks us in a foxhole. Our patrol is now reduced to drifting with the ice.

'Low-energy scouting?'

He grins. 'We are checking where the floes will go and how the wind is moving them – if it will be safe for ships. In two hours this floe will be out of the fairway.' Then he adds, 'In my dream I was going on board another vessel to start work. You should get overtime for working in your sleep.'

We watch the electronic chart, the radar and the J-Map. Tem pulls up a section of the coast. 'This is the *Sisu* buoy. They went the wrong side of it and found a sandbank.'

I trace the outlines of outcrops and islets. 'What do these names mean?'

'One Stone ... Bird Grave ... Up here near Kemi, Murder Island.'

'What happened?'

'A lot is related to the civil war. Kemi is still a Red city, and Tampere.'

It was a particular feature of the 1918 civil war that reprisals were often worse than the battles themselves. Prisoners and combatants attempting to surrender were routinely shot. The Whites implemented a version of ethnic cleansing against Russians – revolutionaries and neutral residents alike – killing them out of hand. The White victory at Varkaus, which gave them the north of the country, saw twenty fatalities during the fight and a hundred and eighty Red prisoners killed after surrendering. When the Finnish state broadcaster Yle asked for memories of the civil war in 2016 it addressed the greatest Finnish silence of them all. A quarter of those responding said the topic was still a sensitive issue in their family. Stories of ruthlessness, guilt and silence were among the respondents' themes, along with pride in combatant grandparents and continued loyalty to their cause.

'My father was a ten-year-old boy in 1918 when they came to fetch his father for execution. He was strongly influenced by this: he lived his entire life as a leftist and communist – a defender of the poor,' said one. The programme's balancing account ran: 'Grandmother remembers when the Red Guard came looking for her father. She crawled through Red ditches with her family to escape. We ingested her message along with our mother's milk: we have never voted for or supported any party or candidate that was Red, socialist or communist.' What stays with me is almost an aside in Yle's commentary on their survey: submissions which spoke of the 'vindictive treatment of orphaned Red children'. If there is a measure of the psychosis of civil war, perhaps this is it. A century later Yle reported that Finnish children are now among the happiest and least dissatisfied on the planet. The contrast is dizzying,

an astounding tribute to the progress of a people, of
a continent, of a world. What miracles we can achieve
in only a hundred years.

Tem is watching a ship heading for the shallows. 'She is
trying to make a run between there,' he says, indicating
two outcrops. 'We keep an eye on her in case anything
strange happens.'

I turn to Arvo. 'Have you ever seen anything weird at
sea? Anything you could not explain?'

'Yes! Fireballs. Meteorites. Strange stuff. If you sit
half of your life here in the dark ... Glowing plankton!'
He mimes rubbing his eyes and grabbing binoculars.

'Are you superstitious?'

'Of course we are!' Arvo cries. His smile has amazement in it – partly at the question, partly at the answer.

'Never sit on a ... thing you tie the ship to?' Ville says
immediately.

'A bollard?'

'Never sit on a bollard. It's unlucky.'

'No whistling,' Arvo says. 'Brings storms.'

'Never light a cigarette from a candle,' says Ville. 'If
you do a sailor drowns.'

Sampo appears, not a superstitious man. 'The striped flags are out today. We have finally legalised gay marriage in Finland!'

'Congratulations! What took you so long?'

'It's embarrassing. The Finns party, you know the True Finns, the right wing? We had a vote in 2014 but then there was a challenge.'

'How are you on immigration?'

'It's an issue. Not for me. I don't mind we have immigrants. I'm more than happy to pay a solidarity tax if my kids have good hospitals and good schools. I'm glad my kids' school is mixed – and immigrants.'

'How is that done?'

'When they built the housing it was deliberately mixed, so the schools are mixed.'

'So simple, again!'

'Yeah. And I like living next to the sprout hippies. I take great pleasure in driving past them in my Silverado ...'

'Sprout hippies?'

'*Ituhippi!*' Tem and Sampo laugh. 'Sprout hippy, vegetarian, green ...'

'It's not quite Norway,' Sampo says to Reidun. 'At your cash points you just put your social security number in and it asks how much you want.'

'That's what you guys are doing,' she says, 'Citizens' wage.'

Sampo is tracking the shortcutting ship. 'How's our hero? She's got a draught of … five metres … and what's she carrying? Phenyls! Oh, so that's OK then. Poisonous to all life but soluble in water! And another one following her, look. Save fuel.'

The ship sits idle in the ice until the light dims to blue-purple. During a walk around the deck a hail of black shot-like soot fires out of the funnel and falls like gravel. Lasse was cleaning the boilers, he says at supper.

'I tell you an engineer's joke. A man jumps out of a plane and his parachute doesn't work, so he tries the reserve parachute. He pulls the cord but it doesn't open. He pulls the cord on his third parachute and that doesn't work either. Just then he sees a man coming up towards him, flying through the sky with no parachute. He says, "Hey, do you know anything about parachutes?" The guy says, "Do you know anything about steam boilers?"' Everyone laughs, and I want to hug them for it, and Lasse for his effort. Lasse takes the applause like a man who has just brought off a card trick as well as it could be done.

You do not have to have Finnish to follow the silences and half-conversations of these gentle, inward men: they do not seem shy so much as withheld, reminiscent of the farmers I know at home, more given to listening than speech. The mid-twentieth century in Finland saw over a million people leave farming and forestry for work in the cities of the south. ('My grandparents were from the country,' Tem told me. 'They moved to the city and changed their name.') Within a few decades half the population was urbanised, a vastly accelerated version of a process which took two centuries elsewhere in Europe. Perhaps the self-reliance of a recently rural people suddenly displaced and re-rooted became self-containment, the heritage of the wilds carried into the noise and crush of the cities.

Just after nightfall, as we leave the ice for Rahja roads, the wind drops and the bay calms. The open water is an invisible void, perfectly still, as though we sail over space. Below us small rafts of ice hover as if on a starless sky. We back a little way into Rahja's channel, clearing it pointlessly, as far as I can tell, then come out again and set course for Kokkola. The approach to our last night's station takes us across a soulful sea where a ship's lamps glow like campfires. The *Patricia V* has completed her loading in the bay. She weighs anchor, her lights spilling shimmering tracks across the black water, and turns south, loaded with seventy-five thousand tonnes of iron ore pellets for Rotterdam. Ville parks us in the ice, in the same foxhole we left two days ago, and the ship falls into peace.

CHAPTER 16

Changeover

'VILLE IS whistling!' Tem cries.

'He wants storms,' Arvo says, making tea.

Tem watches Ville start the engines. *Otso* puffs out a balloon of her thickest, blackest smoke. 'I have never seen this before, but for some reason Ville is happy.'

'How do you feel, Tem?'

'For some reason I am a little bit sad. Happy to be going home but also sad to leave.'

'There are a lot of happy people on this ship!' Arvo declares as we swing towards Kokkola.

Reidun shakes her head. 'Not me. I never like to go home.'

'What will you do, Tem? Have a drink tonight?'

'I don't think so. I will wait; we are taking the children to go skiing this weekend. I will have a drink then. Where we are skiing I will be chauffeuring. There is a place I wait to pick them up. They will ski and I will have coffee, and when they call I will say, "Ye-es?"' He bursts out laughing. 'Ye-es?' is spoken with a rising intonation, a comical mockery of a child's demands.

Dark rain gathers to the west as one gull appears before the foremast, leading us into port. Kokkola harbour is heroically bleak, iron, concrete and machinery in symphony under a low sky. The quay is piled with rust-coloured cones of ore and looped with conveyor belts on stilts. Three cranes are working over *Kumpula*, a dwarfing black and red bulk carrier. 'One of the largest ships in Finland,' Ville says, as we inch through *shuga* towards our berth behind her. *Kumpula*'s lifeboat is set high up behind the bridge on a chute aimed steeply at the water.

'Have you ever been on a free-fall boat?' Ville says. 'I did it on a course. You strap in facing backwards. There is a moment of noise, a moment of silence and then bang, you hit!'

'Did you scream?'

'Sailors are quiet and cool,' he returns.

Now Tem steps up to perform the ritual of manoeuvring *Otso* into her berth.

'The master brings us alongside unless the master is drunk!' Arvo announces. Arvo is a-bustle with energy this morning, his flight connections to the Ålands lined up, his bags packed. Tem slow-juggles the controls, Ville behind him like a coach, concentrating as if on Tem's behalf. This is not quite the silent teaching he gives Arvo, more a silent solidarity. We edge forward and then back, slowly, slowly, tiny touches – *Come on*, I find myself urging *Otso. In a bit, come left for him!* In order to fully disguise any sense of pressure you must also disguise the sense of relief: as the heaving lines are thrown ashore we all let out a breath we did not know we were holding. At 08.09, six minutes early, our gangway touches the quay.

We make our farewells with handshakes (Arvo and Lasse), bashful laughter (Ville and Sampo) and small speeches (Reidun and me). We will keep in touch, we promise. Tem, Reidun and I will share a taxi and a train to Oulu. Tem appears in fawn corduroy and fawn trainers, wheeling a mint-green suitcase. You might guess he was a teacher or a civil servant, but a captain leaving his ship, never. We disembark, slipping over pellets of iron ore the size of fat grapes, frozen in bunches. As the taxi pulls away I turn for the apocryphal Filipino seafarer's favourite view of the ship, framed in the back window. Beside *Kumpula*, *Otso* looks small, neat and impatient, her smart blue and white out of place in her rusty surroundings, her calling clear in her lines. She will be back in the ice tonight.

The drive is solemn. Reidun is dreading work emails. Tem is adjusting; land is a demotion to any captain. I am sorry to leave our mission, our ark apart from the world. Our moods change as we reach the station: the cold is vivifying and cheering; unfamiliar faces seem wonderfully exotic. A long goods train heaves a thousand pine logs northwards, trailing their sap-green scent. The smell is sharp and thrilling and I realise how strange it has been to be within sight of land and utterly apart from it. No scent or sensation that belongs to it has been anywhere near us until now. I want to walk and wade through snow and inhale the Christmas smell of pines, to eat well and slowly, to swim and stretch and hug.

Our train includes a separate compartment, glassed in.

'For people with allergies,' Tem explains.

Hay fever and asthma rates have soared in Finland, as they have throughout the wealthy world, but researchers point to a particular Finnish obsession with scrupulous cleanliness. Everything from tarmacked roads to anti-allergenic rugs is blamed for robbing Finns of their immunity. Over the border in Russian Karelia, where allergy rates are very low, contact with dust, dirt and animals is much more common than in Finland, researchers report. Allergies would seem to be the price of hygiene.

The contrast with grimy, immunity-boosting British trains is fabulous. Finns enjoy cabinets for telephone conversations, self-service tea and coffee and an easy punctuality. Through the windows Ostrobothnia passes in scrolls of birch and pine trunks, white meadows, farms painted pale yellows and greens, horses in rugs and a stillness in the air, snow-lit and soft.

Tem refills his coffee and launches into a round of seafarers' jokes.

'This one is Finnish. The coastguard calls a Swedish ship: "How many persons on board?" "No Perssons, one Jansson!" Because Persson is a Swedish name ...'

'Got it!'

'The coastguard calls again. "Where are you?" "On the bridge." "No, what is your position?" "Second mate!"'

'Classic.'

'"Mayday, Mayday, I am sinking." "What are you thinking?"'

'I surrender!'

'Ha! OK. Look! These are breast-cancer awareness.'

Where a pasture meets the forest are a line of silage bales wrapped in bright pink plastic. We talk of farmers and schools and children; Tem's daughter attends a school which also trains teachers.

'It is quite wonderful,' he says. 'They are taught maths by a Japanese teacher who speaks no Finnish! So the only language is maths.'

For all the health centres, the technology hubs, the effortless transport, the equality and progressive values I have heard and seen and read about, it is this line of Tem's which seems to speak most deeply of Finland: a Japanese teacher and a ten-year-old Finn speaking mathematics to each other. The teacher will be here because Finnish education is among the best in the world, and teachers are accorded a commensurate status in society. In a recent poll of graduates a quarter said teaching was their ideal profession. Instead of piles of tests and homework, Finnish children are given highly trained and motivated teachers, and free education to PhD. At the end of basic education children are evaluated, not tested.

They can take two to four years to complete high school, depending on their progress. I feel something like physical pain thinking of the contrast with education in my country, where children's success is largely determined by their parents' education and address.

'And what do you do with your time, Tem, when they are at school?'

'When it is quiet I collect coins. It's an interesting thing to do. I like British coins, Edwardian and Victorian but also anything before decimalisation. I am always looking for them on the Internet, for the strange ones, but they are very expensive.'

'Why British?'

'The history, the silver coins which actually are silver, shillings and florins. I am interested in them before they were alloys. So when the kids are at school sometimes I am researching and arranging ...'

It casts another light on this man whose shipboard life is constant responsibility, near-constant noise, companionship, motion, decision. For some reason I do not picture Tem the numismatist with music playing or the radio on; rather in peace, working on his hobby in a slip of time.

Maja, Tem's wife, will meet us at Oulu. We are all going out to lunch.

'There are two restaurants, and I have the menus here,' Tem says, producing printouts. 'There is a modern one or a more traditional one.'

We tease him for his efficiency and settle on the traditional.

Tem's phone rings.

'Oh, you are at the port? OK. And do you have a number for the ship? OK, here it is. If you call them they will contact the security. I am on a train now, but you can speak with Seppo – he is the captain – and then they will help you. Oh, I am sorry. Yes. This is the number …' His manner is so soft and mollifying he might be a therapist.

He hangs up. 'The admiral's daughter is stuck at the port gate,' he says.

'The way you deal with people is extraordinary! So gentle …'

'I am always being calm or pretending to be calm.'

Maja stands straight-backed, the inverted V of grey hair in her fringe a striking highlight against blonde, her manner warm and direct. Husband and wife embrace briefly, no fuss, no great homecoming. The restaurant is a log cabin, with red and white checked tablecloths in

the comfortable dim light of dark wood. Maja and Tem
defuse and defer the tension of the approaching holiday
in rapid shorthand: plans for the packing, the kids and
the long drive north are all in hand, and Maja has work
to do before departure. She is a health and safety
inspector now, which means travel all over Finland.

'Do you miss the sea?' I ask.

'No!' She smiles. Then she hesitates. 'Sometimes in
summer I think it could be nice to be out. But no.'

'And you were a rarity out there, a female officer?'

'Yes. You had to be strong. If a man needed help he
could ask, but a woman no, you felt a pressure.'

'A pressure to be better than everyone else?'

'Oh yes! Of course. But I always feel this. On land
too, we always feel this.'

'Sometimes you did not ask for help when you should,
when anybody should,' Tem says.

'Yes,' she returns. 'That is how it is. Anyway I prefer
the land.'

'It seems like a wonderful job, Tem. You would not
change it, would you? Apart from the absences.'

They look at each other.

'The only thing is knowing when he will be free,' Maja
begins.

'You do not know when you are working,' Tem says. 'For some weeks yes, but not for some months.'

'Last year we had to cancel our holiday,' Maja adds. 'They needed him to work.'

'It is the only bad thing in my life,' Tem says. 'I do not know when I will be working and when I will be free. I do not have control of the future.'

A waitress comes for our order. Maja spends a long time detailing allergies; the waitress is confident and reassuring. Waiters and waitresses in Finland are expert in this area, Maja says. 'You know we are all lactose intolerant?'

Tem grins. 'Well, all except me.'

'And you met on a ferry between Holland and Britain?'

'Yes!' Maja laughs. 'Our first date was in Middlesbrough.'

'Did you like Middlesbrough?'

'It was terrible! Do you remember where we went?' she asks Tem.

For the first time in ten days he hesitates. He looks at the menu, with its choices of fish, reindeer, elk and pasta, as if for help.

'It was an Italian ...'

'It was an Indian! Do you remember what we had?'

'Yesss … It was … spicy.'

'It was chicken curry!'

'Yes! I know it had lots of rice. Yes.'

She laughs and rolls her eyes. 'He wasn't thinking of the food.' Reidun laughs. 'This is good!'

'And you were his senior officer, Maja?'

'Yes!' She looks at her husband with a sweet affection. 'He made his reports to me.'

'It was twice as hard,' Tem says, meeting her gaze. 'The first date *and* she was the boss. And it's been that way ever since.'

It is snowing when we leave, heavy wet flakes skidding sidelong through grey air. The temperature is only a little below freezing.

'I hate it when it is warm like this,' Maja says. 'It will be better at the weekend, minus ten, minus fifteen – no slush. Everyone is happier when it is really cold.'

She has a report to write. We drop her at her office. There is no question of Reidun and me taking a taxi to the airport, they insist.

'We have time for me to show you something,' Tem declares, spinning the car through the snow. He drives us to a suburb of tall houses separated by stands of birch trees.

'There,' he says. 'That is ours.'

It is a grand yellow house girt with sheds and a snowy garden, set about with winter light. I am hoping for a look at the coin collection, but there is no time. We drive around the block and set off again.

'Beautiful house, Tem!'

'It's a great area for children,' Reidun says.

'Yes. These houses were built for the veterans of the war.'

'Does the war still matter to people here?'

'I would say it is not forgotten,' Tem says. 'You know Finns used to shake boxes of matches at the Germans? Rovaniemi! They burned the town when they left, but this is only history now.'

He shakes his right fist as he drives, rattling invisible matches, an unexpected burst of not-altogether-staged feeling from this most pacific of men. Tem is a slightly different person on land, already in paternal mode, answering questions like a father, eyes on the traffic, an ear on the conversation, thoughts stretching ahead to the reunion with his children.

* * *

At the airport Tem embraces Reidun and shakes my hand. Reidun is in low spirits, the backlog of messages on her phone nagging her and nothing else to do at the airport but begin to answer them.

'You can always come back!' Tem tells her, and she says he must come to Norway, and we all make sure we have each other's emails. Reidun and I thank our captain.

'It is my pleasure,' he says. 'If you ever want to come back, *Otso* will be waiting.'

Reidun takes the Oslo flight, and I prepare for a marathon to Helsinki, London, Manchester and on into the Pennines, where I will arrive at 4 a.m. Finnish time. The departure area offers daybeds, wooden armchairs and an atmosphere more like a communal drawing room than an airport. Commuters queue for beer as a text comes from Katri: 'I am drunk already and going dancing!' The spirit of old-fashioned seafaring is most alive in the youngest of the crew.

I watch the other passengers: two American men joking about the banking business, a professorial Finn on his phone, an elderly man thinking about his family, by his contemplative half-smile, a smart woman my age who swigs down Prosecco like water; all of us suspended in the in-between time that travel simultaneously grants and steals.

My notebook lists the cargoes we escorted. There was zinc concentrate from Sweden and coal from Poland, calcium chloride for Sweden and iron ore for Bremen, zinc for Rostock, fertiliser for Lübeck and pyritic ashes for Rotterdam. There were the wind turbines for Rahja and Raahe; there were containers from Hamburg and containers to Hamburg. There was caustic soda for Kotka. From these cargoes will come food, cars, buildings, paper, light, heat and power, the fundamentals of civilisation. But the view from *Otso* does not extend to abstract horizons. The crew's care over their work is professional, and as Sampo and Ville expressed it, also a matter of national pride. To the ships of the world coming up into the ice of Bothnia, *Otso* is the first manifestation of Finland after the voices on the radio. While most civilian vessels fly flags of convenience, *Otso*'s blue and white livery is a projection of Finnish expertise, Finnish robustness and Finnish prowess. For observers of geopolitics icebreakers are an emblem of not entirely soft power. China's *Snow Dragon* is used to demonstrate a national interest in the north polar region (in 1999 she turned up unannounced in the Canadian Arctic, panicking the authorities, who had not seen her coming), as are Russia's expanding fleet and the icebreakers of Canada and Sweden. Finland's ship-yards are busy with Russian orders for the next gener-ation of vessels. Designed with asymmetric hulls, they will skid sideways into the pack, opening channels wide enough for tankers. To the local travellers filing into the plane now, boarding a Finnair jet (majority-owned by the state) at a Finavia airport (wholly owned by the state), the voyages of *Otso* are another beat in the rhythm of Finland's daily tune, a flap of the flag, 'Some little bit,' as Jouni the engineer described his morning's work, some little, vital bit.

Last night I dreamed of the ice; there were narwhals in it, basking sharks and seals, all frozen into a kind of porcelain. The voyage of *Otso* broke a heaven and a horror out from my internal sea. The horror was a glimpse of a world in which humans are almost the only creatures, our machines the only life. A seal and eagle on the first day, three crows, two gulls, a raven, another two seals – in ten days! It is the longest I have ever been anywhere with so little sight of birds or animals. The mid-Pacific and the Karakum Desert are teeming places compared to this frozen sea. The absence of life seemed a foreboding. Our lot in a world denuded of other creatures would be a deep and dreadful existential loneliness. Imagine having no other companionship than humans and whatever we tame or breed: no wild thing, no bird to make the sky surround it, no flourish of being in landscape, no iteration of spirit in form.

Though this was only a reflection of the season – in the spring there will be seals and sea eagles; the Bay of Bothnia still sustains salmon, pike, perch, sea-spawning grayling and sea trout – there was a shuddering emptiness in a world which seemed only elemental.

That emptiness, for all its magnificence, peopled itself with ghosts, some enchanting, some eerie. In Charles Bonnet syndrome an active brain, underserved by a decaying optic nerve, fills the mind with apparently visual phantasmagoria. There were moments when something similar seemed to happen to me. Faced with the ice and sky, the circling and the waiting, tightness in my stomach

became a parade of fears, strange doubts and premon-
itions – phenomena hitherto always banished by travelling
and writing. It felt and still feels frightening, but there
must be a healthy scourging in it, a kind of sauna of
confinement and intensity, wringing toxins out of the
mind's pores.

The sauna, even the ship's stripped-back version,
without whipping birch twigs or snow rolling, made
sense of the proverbial Finnish injunction to behave
there as you would in church. You settle into yourself
as the heat rises until you pass a point of thinking and
begin to leave yourself behind. As in a meditation, the
last directed thoughts are of your breath and body,
each tippling bead of sweat a wriggly kind of pleasure
as you imagine and feel it bearing afflictions away. In
a steaming cupboard in the bowels of a ship in the
middle of an ice floe somewhere in the darkness
between Finland and Sweden a naked man saw himself
for a second as if from far above, a comically tiny fleck
communing with the universe from this position of
pure eccentricity. I put down my notebook and laughed.
Sacrilege to have brought it here, though I think my
friend Thomas would have approved. The voyage came

about partly through his legacy, which connected Pekka at the embassy and me. He was an iconoclast and a wonderful, comical scourge, whose help and advice often came wrapped in mockery. The idea of a fool like me seeking self-improvement by sitting in a hot box off Ostrobothnia with a notebook would have made him laugh.

Travelling with Finnish seafarers was a lesson in considered and gentle self-possession. Often, watching from the bridge as we voyaged through darkness and snow, my thoughts quietened to a kind of listening silence, a wordless companionship with the navigators. Working and watching through the small hours out in that obscure gulf was like being admitted to an almost secret society, unseen and benevolent, which stands guard over every night.

From Oulu to Helsinki, to the late pulsing streets of London, to the last train and finally home, I brought a souvenir of the voyage in a double feeling which has been settling and crystallising as I have written its story.

There is *Otso*'s mighty bow, thrusting forward over the ice, which is snowed and jumbled on the surface,

consolidated pack stretching away beyond the searchlights. And there is a sickle of a crack running forward,
curving away from the ship, shooting out more shatter
lines, every splinter evidence of our power and efficacy.
How mighty is our roaring attack! The decks shudder,
the impacts grate and crash, and the pack splits, barely
hindering our charge. The confrontation is never an
equal contest.

Our purpose was destruction, but there was no
benefit to us in final victory. All the while we wished
the weather colder; we wished that more ice would
form. Though the crew relished rest and the abeyance
of that juddering contact, something in us – which was
explicit in Sampo and Ville – also longed for our
opponent to offer more defiance. This double impulse
seemed a portrait in miniature of a particular relationship with nature and the earth. The more deeply buried
its treasures, the vaster its oceans and the more mighty
its resistance, the greater the invention and the reso-
lution earth has drawn from us. From the Pliocene
until now, until this fractional instant of geological
time, earth has been matchless. But now, suddenly, its
opposition is wilting.

The planet threatens to become soggy, tempestuous and backward as the ghost-climates of older worlds are disinterred and loosed again. Perhaps this partly explains our ongoing rapacity, our ever more frenzied extraction and the feebleness of our plans for change. It is as if we are disappointed in the earth, like adolescents struggling to accept a parent's vulnerability. Can it really be so sensitive? Is the ice so thin? It seems to be harder for humankind to nurse a wounded opponent than to battle one still vigorous. But it is touching and revealing that even icebreakers practise conservation. According to Tem's report on the Kemi-Tornio fairway, pristine ice is husbanded there, an unbroken lane which can be used at the season's end, so that ships are not trapped in *shuga* of their own making.

And then there was the heaven, the brightest spell I will remember from the Bay of Bothnia, the privilege and amazement of standing on the sea. A spiral of scribbles on the page of the bay, the plot of *Otso*'s voyage could have belonged to salvagers or treasure hunters searching for the Sampo of the *Kalevala*, that miraculous world-making mill. We seemed to find it that sparkling day when we stepped from the ship onto the ice in a storm of light.

The discovery that the sea really was made solid gave me a fizzing exhilaration. I jumped on the ice as if to test it, trying to land lightly, laughing with delight. If it was familiar to the crew it was a miracle to me that all the air was scintillant, that the horizon was a weld-flash of ice and sky, that distance could only be measured in colour until colour dissolved into glare. Our little bright-suited figures were slow blobs, laughable and laughing. Light poured down and up at once. In the silent vortex of the albedo I felt a mingling of calm and wonder, as if all superfluity had been whipped away. While standing on a mountain top grants you the vista of a scoop of space, from valley bottom to cloud level and beyond, standing on the sea under clear air erases depth and height. The sky begins in the snow under your boots. You are simultaneously huge and as tiny as a fleck.

The stillness of the air held a charge in it, for nothing around us was stable – between the sun and the frigid air creation and destruction were in whirling play. On the underside of the ice below us congelation growth thickened the crystal layers, while in the ridges of our footprints radiation tickled them minutely away. Although you could not hear it or see it, you could not help but sense it, a molecular dance, a duel, an effervescence at the edge of perception: the making and melting of ice.

Acknowledgements

HUGE THANKS, Pekka Isosomppi, for your inspiration and your efforts, which sent me on this voyage. Thank you, Minttu Taajamo and Eero Hokkanen, for all the time and trouble you took in arranging my travels so beautifully.

Great thanks to the crew of *Otso*, superbly led by Teemu Alstela, for your wonderful welcome and endless patience. Thank you especially, Sampo Viherialehto, Ville Suni, Arvo Kovanen, Lasse Matilainen and Reidun Myklebust for your excellent company and kind instruction.

Thank you, the best of the best, Zoe Waldie and Rosie Price at RCW, for your ceaseless encouragement, care and insight, and for finding the book a perfect home with the great ship Chatto and its magnificent captain, Clara Farmer.

Thank you especially Becky Hardie, superb editor, for your marvellous work on the manuscript. (Any infelicities which still afflict it are my doing; all those that do not were exorcised by Becky with unfailing good humour and efficiency.)

I am hugely grateful to Charlotte Humphery for seeing the book through to publication, to Hugh Davis and Anthony Hippisley for their scrutiny of copy and proofs, to designer Julia Connolly and illustrator Eoin Ryan for making this a beautiful object, and to Anna Redman for taking it to the world.

Researching Finland and the Finns sent me on an idiosyncratic journey through libraries and texts. I am particularly indebted to the writings of Jonathan Clements, whose works on Mannerheim and Finnish history and culture make delightful and entertaining points of departure for anyone interested in Suomi.

This book was written through a hard time. My love and deepest thanks to Rebecca Shooter, Aubrey Shooter Clare, Jennifer – on behalf of all of us, Jenny! – Gerald, Emma and Chris Shooter, and to Sally, Alexander and John Clare for your love and support. For unfaltering friendship and kindness, thank you Roger Couhig, Merlin Hughes, Richard Coles, Anna Gavalda, Jay Griffiths, Niall Griffiths, Debs Jones, Douglas Field, Ellie Hunt, Phil O'Farrell, Emma Back, Mike Fuller, Rupert Crisswell, Kartika Panwar, Laura Barton, Dan Richards, Robert Macfarlane, Jeff Young, Andrew MacMillan, Robert Graham, Sarah Maclennan, Helen Tookey, Marge Mather, Alison Finch, Sîan Walker and Henny Schoonderwoerd.

Special thanks to Robin Tetlow-Shooter. Much love xx

penguin.co.uk/vintage